# CHECKPOINT

# CHECKPOINT

•

# CHECK

.

# P O I N T

# Nicholson Baker

Chatto & Windus
LONDON

Published by Chatto & Windus in 2004

First published in the United States of America in 2004 by Knopf

2 4 6 8 10 9 7 5 3 1

First published in Great Britain in 2004 by
Chatto & Windus
Random House, 20 Vauxhall Bridge Road,
London SW1V 2SA

Random House Australia (Pty) Limited
20 Alfred Street, Milsons Point, Sydney,
New South Wales 2061, Australia

Random House New Zealand Limited
18 Poland Road, Glenfield,
Auckland 10, New Zealand

Random House (Pty) Limited
Endulini, 5A Jubilee Road, Parktown 2193, South Africa

The Random House Group Limited Reg. No. 954009
www.randomhouse.co.uk

A CIP catalogue record for this book is available from the British Library

ISBN 0 7011 7819 1

Papers used by Random House are natural,
recyclable products made from wood grown in sustainable forests;
the manufacturing processes conform to the environmental
regulations of the country of origin

Printed and bound in Great Britain by
Bookmarque Ltd, Croydon, Surrey

*For Carroll,*
*and in memory of Bob*

# CHECKPOINT

•

*May 2004*
*Adele Hotel and Suites*
*Washington, D.C.*

JAY: Testing, testing. Testing. Testing.

BEN: Is it working?

JAY: I think so. [*Click . . . click, click.*] Yes, see the little readout? Where'd you get it?

BEN: Circuit City.

JAY: Three hundred and ninety minutes. That should definitely do it. I'll pay you back.

BEN: No, it's fine, honestly.

JAY: Well, thanks, man. I just feel I have a lot in my noggin right now.

BEN: So I gather. You look good, Jay.

JAY: Really? I was working on a fishing boat for a while, dropped some pounds. Are those new glasses?

BEN: Yeah, Julie helped me pick them. Did you know Brooks Brothers made glasses frames?

JAY: No, I did not. Let me see them.

BEN: Sure.

JAY: "Made in China." I always check. Anyway, they suit you. Really, you look less like a bird.

BEN: I'm glad to hear it. So tell me what's up.

JAY: Oh, let's see. Where to begin? Where to begin?

BEN: Obviously you have something on your mind.

JAY: That's true.

BEN: You could begin with that.

JAY: Okay. Uh, I'm going to—okay, I'll just say it. Um.

BEN: What is it?

JAY: I'm going to assassinate the president.

BEN: What do you mean?

JAY: Take his life.

BEN: You're shitting me, right?

JAY: No.

BEN: Tell me this is one of your little flippancies.

JAY: It's not a flippancy.

BEN: Come on, Jay. This isn't—turn that off.

JAY: No, I'd like it on. Before I do it I want to explain, for the record.

BEN: Please turn that off right now.

JAY: It's got to stay on.

BEN: I think I better go.

JAY: Already?

BEN: Yes already. You're talking about the president, am I right? That is what you said. Or did I just hallucinate?

JAY: No, that is what I said. But you can't go.

BEN: This isn't what I thought you were calling me about. I thought maybe your girlfriend had left you.

JAY: She did.

BEN: Well, okay. That's more like it.

JAY: But I also have this plan that I need to execute. Calm down, will you?

BEN: That's pretty funny.

JAY: What?

BEN: You're telling me to calm down when you've got this . . . deed on your mind. It's a major, major, major crime. It doesn't get much more major.

JAY: I know, and it's high time, too. I haven't felt this way about any of the other ones. Not Nixon, not Bonzo, even. For the good of humankind.

BEN: Do you have a gun?

JAY: I don't like guns.

BEN: But do you have one?

JAY: I may.

BEN: That is so low. You're a civilized person.

JAY: Not anymore.

BEN: You can't—the country has no need for this service.

JAY: I think it does. I think we have to lance the fucking boil.

BEN: No, I'm serious, he'll be out of power eventually. Either he loses and he's out, or he wins, and then he's out a little later. Either way, his time will pass in a twinkling. Many years from now you'll be reading the comics in some café somewhere, and you'll think, Boy oh boy, I'm sure glad I didn't do that.

JAY: I'm going to do it today.

BEN: Let's just set it aside, shall we? Just put that off to one side. You know you'll never get away with it. They'll shoot you full of bullets and you'll die. Or they'll fry you. Seriously, you'll die. And for what? Do you know what a bullet does?

JAY: It tears into your flesh at high speed. It rips through your vitals.

BEN: If you get hit here? Half-digested material leaks out of your intestines into your abdominal cavity.

JAY: That's what happened to McKinley.

BEN: You mean President McKinley?

JAY: Yes.

BEN: Well, right. Do you want that to happen to you? They have snipers up on the roof.

JAY: I know, I've seen them. They've got missile launchers up there, too.

BEN: Those guys want to put bullets into you.

JAY: They don't know about me.

BEN: Oh, but they know that there are bad people out there.

JAY: That's true, and I'm one of them.

BEN: I don't think so.

JAY: No, Ben, this guy is beyond the beyond. What he's done with this war. The murder of the innocent. And now the prisons. It's too much. It makes me so angry. And it's a new kind of anger, too. There was a story a year ago, April last year. It was a family at a checkpoint. Do you remember?

BEN: I'm not sure.

JAY: It was a family fleeing in a car. The mother was one of the few survivors. And she said, "I saw—" Sorry. I can't.

BEN: It's all right.

JAY: I'm not going to let him get away with this.

BEN: You think this is all him? What about, you

know, Cheney? What about Donald? What about all the generals who came up with the attack plans? And the hopheads who flew the airplanes?

JAY: *Hey hey, ho ho—George Bush has got to go.*

BEN: Look, he's going to go, it's inevitable, he'll have a successor.

JAY: Now. He has to go now.

BEN: Set it aside. Just set it off to one side, please, will you? What have you been up to?

JAY: Oh, I've had a bunch of jobs. I got into a slight financial scrape.

BEN: How bad?

JAY: Well, I nearly had to declare personal— insolvency, shall we say.

BEN: Ouch.

JAY: It was intense.

BEN: I bet.

JAY: So I've been working as a day laborer.

BEN: You haven't been teaching at all?

JAY: That kind of ended. It was really a part-time thing, anyway, so . . . But the day labor has been really good for me. When you do gruntwork for hours and hours you actually have a lot of mental time.

BEN: Mm.

JAY: Your body is working and your brain can kind of cruise here and there.

BEN: Yeah, I find in the evenings, like when I'm chopping up a cucumber to make salad, that rhythmic *chop, chop, chop,* sometimes I think of a little connection that didn't occur to me all day.

JAY: So tell me how your book is coming.

BEN: Which one? You mean the one—

JAY: The one about the government department during the war, the department that steamed open the envelopes.

BEN: Oh, the Office of Censorship, right. Well, I kind of hit a retaining wall with that one. But we don't need to talk about that.

JAY: I want to. It sounded very interesting when you told me about it.

BEN: Well, okay, I spent some time at the National Archives and then I went to Wisconsin, and I spent some time there, that's where some of the papers are, and, well, the material hasn't started to sing to me yet. But it will, it will.

JAY: When did we last get together? Was that three years ago?

BEN: May have been. Long time.

JAY: I'm so sorry about that wheelbarrow, man.

BEN: No no no.

JAY: I felt bad, I just didn't see it in the dark.

BEN: It's fine, it still works. It lists a little, that's all.

JAY: Really sorry. So what have you been working on instead?

BEN: Instead of what?

JAY: Instead of the book about the steaming open of the envelopes.

BEN: Oh, a few things—a few Cold War themes that I've been pursuing. And my classes take up time—I co-teach an honors seminar every spring.

JAY: Some good students?

BEN: A few. Oh, and I bought a camera! That's my big news.

JAY: A camera, huh? Digital?

BEN: Well, I have a digital camera, but no, this one that I bought is a film camera. It's called a Bronica—a Bronica GS-1.

JAY: A Bronica GS-1. What's that?

BEN: It's a big heavy camera, it uses a wider kind of film.

JAY: Where's it made? Germany?

BEN: No, no, Japan.

JAY: Oh, of course. And it's heavy, is it?

BEN: Yeah, but the great thing is, you don't have

to use a tripod. You can hold it with a handle called a speed grip. I love it.

JAY: It sounds very professional.

BEN: Oh, it's definitely professional—I mean, I'm just an amateur, but it's a privilege to hold this thing. I bought a couple of lenses for it, a beautiful hundred-and-ten-millimeter macro lens, butter smooth. I'm really into lenses now.

JAY: Remember that photograph of the girl, the girl running?

BEN: What girl?

JAY: The girl in Vietnam running from the napalm? She's naked, she's crying.

BEN: Oh, yeah, yeah.

JAY: Well, they've used napalm in Iraq.

BEN: I may have heard something about that.

JAY: Right off the bat they used it. At first they denied it. It came out in a newspaper. Napalm bombs. And some PR guy from the Pentagon wrote an outraged response. "We did NOT use napalm, we got rid of our stocks of napalm years ago, this is a GROSS INACCURACY and a DISSERVICE TO YOUR READERS," and so on and so on. Well, then, of course, it turns out that, well, uh, yes, they're shooting missiles full of this goop that starts intense fires and, well, yes, they're using it to burn people alive, and, uh, yes, all our Army commanders do call it napalm, but it isn't technically napalm because it's not *naphtha-poly-toly-moly-doodlemate,* whatever. Whatever the formula was when they first invented it back behind the stadium.

BEN: The stadium.

JAY: The Harvard stadium. That's where they invented it. So this is a different chemical formula, but the people who shoot the missiles call it napalm, the generals call it napalm, because hey, it's exploding globs of fiery jelly that cause an agonizing death. In fact, it's improved fire jelly—it's even harder to put out than the stuff they used in Vietnam. And Korea. And Germany. And Japan. It just has another official name. Now it's called Mark 77. I mean, have we learned nothing? Mark 77! I'm going to kill that bastard.

BEN: No you're not.

JAY: Penisfucker!

BEN: Jay, relax.

JAY: Why should I relax? Jiminy Cricket. Anyway. So you bought a camera, did you? How diverting. How much did you spend?

BEN: It doesn't matter.

JAY: Look, we're having a talk. You tell me you

bought a camera. I say that that's glorious news, and I ask you how much it was.

BEN: I got it used.

JAY: I see, so it was probably cheaper than it would have been had you gotten it new, am I right?

BEN: Yes.

JAY: How much cheaper?

BEN: Oh, it cost me, let's see, about twelve hundred for the body and the macro lens.

JAY: Whoa, not that cheap.

BEN: Yeah, and then I got a wide-angle lens for another six hundred, and another lens after that, and I got an extension tube coming, so it continues.

JAY: Boy, that's serious money. You know I sold my car last week? I got eighteen hundred dollars for it. Of course the hood kept flying up in my face. "All right, where's the road?" But I'm sure your camera is worth it. And your "speed grip."

BEN: Well, you can get some amazing deals right now, because everybody's panicking and dumping their film cameras so that they can raise enough money to buy one of those super-expensive digital cameras.

JAY: I thought film was dead.

BEN: It's dying, but it isn't dead. The larger

formats still hold more detail. Look, my friend, look. Okay, they used napalm. That's very bad. I agree. Shooting the head of state is not a solution.

JAY: I don't like guns.

BEN: What are you, a swordsman? Are you going to flip a dagger into him?

JAY: No.

BEN: Are you going to blow up the White House?

JAY: Of course not; think of the innocent people. That's what *they* would do. In fact, that's what they did do.

BEN: So—how were you planning on doing it?

JAY: Couple of ways. I've got some radio-controlled flying saws, they look like little CDs but they're ultrasharp and they're totally deadly, really nasty.

BEN: Deadly nasty saws.

JAY: They're incredible, lethal as hell. And a few other avenues of effort going forward, as well. I've got a huge boulder I'm working on that has a giant ball bearing in the center of it so that it rolls wherever I tell it to. And it's indestructible. It's made of depleted uranium and it's a hundred tons of metal that just *rolls,* baby. So that's an option.

BEN: You're going to squash the president?

JAY: If I have to, I will. I met this inventor at a bar in Nahant. This guy is brilliant. He came up with the aimable saws, and if anything he's more upset with the war than I am, so he's not about to sell his inventions to the military.

BEN: So—where's all this gear? I didn't see any big boulders parked in the entrance when I came in.

JAY: You know that you can almost see the White House from this window? See that little tuft of trees there? I think it's just to the right of that. Right there. I have some unusual bullets, too.

BEN: You know, you're getting me nervous.

JAY: I'm getting myself nervous. Yesterday I walked around looking at all the people, wondering who's a staffer, who's a lobbyist. All these earnest faces. Parts of Washington are so beautiful, the Capitol Building, I mean, wow, that thing is stately. Big dome sitting on top of it. Then looking down over the Mall. A lot of money expended on that Lincoln Monument. And then you've got the White House, a little over to one side. And in your mind you have this piece of dark mischief, and you wonder if people can tell.

BEN: Oh, brother.

JAY: The problem is that the real elements that are moving Washington are not on the Mall. The

Department of Defense is off across the river in that huge fortress, that brain-warper of a building. Five sides. It's like it's intentionally made to drive you over the edge just thinking about it.

BEN: Don't think about it.

JAY: Wolfowitz is there. I mean, what's up with him? And then the CIA over in McLean, Virginia.

BEN: "The truth shall make you free." You know they've got that chiseled in the marble of the lobby?

JAY: No, I didn't. And then all the consulting companies and the big federal departments out in Silver Spring, and Alexandria, Virginia, and Bethesda, and all these places. Spread out all over, far as the eye can see.

BEN: That's deliberate, that they're spread out. The whole beltway idea—

JAY: Yeah, so what you have in downtown Washington is this artificial image of a capital city. You've got the grandeur, you've got the art museums, the Hirshhorn, the Smithsonian, the Natural History Museum, you've got the museum of the African American, you've got the museum of the Native American—gee whiz, kids, this is the United States of America! And then you've got this unelected fucking drunken OILMAN over there squatting in the house itself. Muttering over his prayer book every morning. Then he gives the order to invade. That's how this began, you know.

BEN: How it began? Why don't you tell me.

JAY: Do you really want to know, or are you just being therapeutic with me?

BEN: I don't care. You don't have to tell me anything. You called me up. I'm here.

JAY: But do you want to know?

BEN: Sure, I want to know. Yes.

JAY: Well, so last year, I marched on the White House. This was at the very beginning of the war. First they had a tip that Saddam was in a certain house, so they sent in that cruise missile to kill him. But, oopsie, he wasn't there—yet another totally illegal assassination bungled by the CIA. And then, I think it was the next day, there was the huge attack on all the palaces. Not military targets. Against the Geneva Conventions.

BEN: "Decapitation." I remember.

JAY: So just after that, I took a bus here, because there was supposed to be a big march on the White House. There was going to be an even bigger march in New York City, too, but I wanted to be in the place where the crime was being committed. To assign blame, you know? I felt there was nothing else to do. All the reasonable arguments against an attack had already been made, all the op-ed pieces had been written. It didn't seem to matter. There was bloodlust in the air and there was a thrilled feeling that it was all inevitable. "Let's see what happens!" So the planes went in, and the missiles went in, and all I had left to do was to come here and shout till my voice stopped working. That's all I could do.

BEN: Yeah, we—

JAY: And there were all these cops on horseback that came trotting briskly, mounties, all lined up, self-important mounties, with blank faces. We were just a bunch of people with signs who wanted to march to the White House and shout that the president was a war criminal, but the funny thing is that nowadays here you can't march to the White House, you're really not allowed anywhere near the White House, they've got things blocked off and this maze of barriers around, so all you can do is pretend that you're marching on the White House when actually the house itself is way way off in the middle distance, and you're in a little sort of park, with your sign in the air, standing there.

BEN: What did your sign say?

JAY: "Murderers."

BEN: Ah.

JAY: So then the crowd started to get bigger and we poured out into the street, and then it became kind of interesting because the horse cops were trying to keep three different phalanxes of gathering protesters apart, but we just *oozed*, man, we were like a huge amoeba of dissent and we poured around the block from one side and then another side and suddenly we were in front of the horse cops and behind them and coming in from the right, and they looked kind of silly there—because what were they blocking?

BEN: Nothing.

JAY: And then the motorcycle cops came, about a hundred of them, with those low-slung panniers. I don't mind the sunglasses and the engine-revving, it's part of their act, but some of them drove down the sidewalks at forty miles an hour, freaking people out. The crowd had gotten big by then.

BEN: You were pulling in people.

JAY: Yeah, we were pulling in people, it was a spontaneous surge of humanity, because we were so furious about that bombing. It was so obviously terror bombing—and I didn't even know about the napalm then. There were government employees marching—I overheard them saying, "Keep your head down so they can't take a picture." And there was one guy, oh, he stood up against an equestrian statue, and he was holding a small white sign, right in front of his chest—it said SEE YOU IN THE HAGUE, MR. BUSH.

BEN: Good one.

JAY: I thought, Right on, right on. And I shouted stuff that I never would have believed that I would shout. My voice was destroyed by the end of the day, I was just croaking. "Stop the violence! Stop the hate!"

BEN: That's called peaceful protest. Julie and I—

JAY: Oh, it was really something, for about an hour in the middle they had us caught, walled off between two streets, with rows of Plexiglas shields and nightsticks and paddy wagons—and I just thought, Man, all we want to say today is, This attack is wrong, so get the shit out of our way, you shitassing bluebeards, so we can just *say* this. But actually, you know what?

BEN: What?

JAY: They were very restrained, they were. I've heard things about Washington cops, but this really wasn't bad. Their jaw muscles were jumping, some of them were angry, but they held back. And some of them beeped their little motorcycle horns in rhythm when we were chanting.

BEN:  Did they really?

JAY:  Oh, that made us cheer. And any time somebody flashed a peace sign from a window or a roof we would cheer, I mean it really felt straightforwardly democratic, and there were no bloody incidents, one or two guys got a little testy and they were wrestled down and hauled off, but we were standing there in front of the Plexiglas shields, and, you know? I had nothing really in common with all these people I was marching with—I'm not actually, you know, if you really want to know, pro-choice, for instance. In fact, quite the contrary.

BEN:  Hmm.

JAY:  This war, Ben? Is an abortion. It's an abortion performed on a whole country. I mean in some ways I'm actually surprisingly conservative, if you get down to it. But there I was with my fist in the air, I'm sobbing, I'm screaming with these people because we all sensed and we knew, regardless of what we did or didn't have in common in other ways, we all knew that the war that the United States was waging on that patchwork country was, was—it was ushering a new kind of terribleness into the world. And we knew that we had to do something. So we marched and marched and marched, and we shouted till we couldn't shout anymore, and then we all went home and we put on our pajamas or our whatevers, and we went to sleep and woke up the next morning, and what? People were still getting their limbs blown off—families were still being killed. I'd given it everything I had. I felt like a lump of depleted uranium.

BEN: Well, you'd walked all day.

JAY: Yeah, oh, and at the end all the cops were lined up in a long long row to keep us from going into a certain park, and as I passed I thanked them, I said, Thank you, thank you, thank you, thank you, nodding to each one of them, because they had been restrained, and there hadn't been any violence, and that's something. That's really important.

BEN: So you thanked them.

JAY: I did, and the next day, when I woke up, I told myself you're not going to read blogs all day. Because I'd been reading Daily Kos and the Agonist, Talking Points Memo, checking Google News twenty times a day.

BEN: I don't read blogs so much.

JAY: I said to myself, No more, because where does that get you? You've got to detach. It's happening no matter what you do, no matter how well informed or not informed you are. And I lay there in this big house where I was staying, listening to myself breathe, not moving my head, just blinking. That's when it happened. There was an old *National Geographic* map of the solar system on the wall near the bed, and it was just when the sun was coming into the room in a certain way, so that the sun hit one of the pushpins that was holding a corner of it, a lower corner, to the wall, and there was a moment when this yellow pushpin shined out. It was as if at that moment the pushpin was a celestial body. And I thought, The solar system, man, now that's neutral, it's eternal, you can't politicize it, it's on a different scale or plane, and I found that that was quite a comforting idea. The remoteness of the planets. The fact that the sunlight had come ninety-three million miles down through space and into that window just in order to light up the end of a pushpin—and I was thinking all this in a kind of peaceful way. . . . Is this working?

BEN: I think so, you could check it again.

[*Click, click.*]

JAY: Good, because—well, anyway, I thought, it doesn't matter to the solar system what my status is. It doesn't matter to, say, the Oort cloud whether I'm in jail or dead or alive, and it doesn't matter whether the president is dead or alive. You see? It's a matter of complete indifference to the universe at large.

BEN: Uh-oh.

JAY: So anyway, I had a moment of clarity, that's all. Just a moment of understanding that I was capable of something that I didn't know that I was capable of. That was all last year. And then he was on the aircraft carrier with that freaky flight suit on, and it was supposedly over, and then there was the Sunni Triangle, and the "insurgents," you know, death everywhere, and now it's all ramping up again, there's a new massing of forces. And I know I'm capable of it.

BEN: You're scaring me, man. Let me see your pupils. I have a feeling that you're going back to the bad time. Are you?

JAY: No, now that was totally different. That was a simple dispute.

BEN: Sawing the legs off the chair of the assistant principal?

JAY: The man took joy in persecuting people. And the sawing made a valid point. People thanked me. Anyway, very different situation. What I mean is, that day that I marched taught me a lot, and I think by doing it I was pushed beyond some inner barrier of restraint. Have you taken a look at Ellsberg's book?

BEN: You mean Ellsberg as in the Pentagon Papers?

JAY: Yeah, I saw him on C-SPAN, too. He's so smart, and I think he really is someone to admire. He goes to a peace conference and there's this Harvard kid there—this is in the late sixties—and the kid is talking about how he's going to go to jail soon and how that's the best thing that he and the other kids can do to protest the war is to fill up the jails, and Ellsberg goes into the bathroom, goes into a stall, and he sits there for an hour crying because he says to himself, This is the best thing that our children can do, the best hope that this Harvard kid can have? Is that he can go to jail? And he says to himself, We're eating our young. And that's when he made the decision. And those Pentagon Papers, man, they are so bloated with old wrongs, under Kennedy, under Johnson. Just an ever-blooming flowerbed of evil.

BEN: You know that on the Net you can listen now to Nixon and Kissinger talking on the phone the very day the Pentagon Papers came out?

JAY: Nixon and Kissinger, really?

BEN: Nixon and Richard Helms, too, but there are some long beeps in that one. I think it's at the

National Security Archive. Kissinger and Nixon talk about how many soldiers have died, and then Kissinger says something like, "Vat the papers make clear, Mr. President, is that it didn't start vith you but vith Kennedy and Johnson." Which is certainly true.

JAY: The point is that you reach a moment when a different kind of action is necessary, and I've reached that point.

BEN: Well, now, Daniel Ellsberg sent a bunch of Xerox copies to some newspapers. You're talking about something very different. Very different. You're talking about suddenly leaping onto the world stage. You don't have any idea what you might set in motion, what kind of uproar, what kind of clamping down would follow. There's no way to predict. You want this wastebasket of a man to become a martyr?

JAY: Just listen to me a little.

BEN: I'll listen, but you see I'm in a bit of a pickle now. If you then go do this, or attempt to do this—because, believe me, you will fail if you try—but if you attempt it, then I become an accessory.

JAY: I hate that legal language. Skip it, skip it.

BEN: What I should be doing is picking up the phone and calling the Justice Department and saying, "Um, Mr. Ashcroft, there's this guy I know who may need to go to Guantánamo Bay for a while and cool down. No, he doesn't need a lawyer."

JAY: You wouldn't do that.

BEN: Maybe I should, though.

JAY: If you picked up the phone, I might pull out a gun.

BEN: I don't think you would.

JAY: I might—I might well. And I might threaten you with it.

BEN: I just don't think that that's in your nature.

JAY: And when you saw the gun, you would put the phone down. Wouldn't you?

BEN: Yes.

JAY: And because I'd threatened you with the gun, with an actual physical bullet—not a bullet in the stomach or the head, of course, but a bullet, say, in the lower leg—it would stop our conversation, because it's a violent threat, and I would ask you to leave, and you would leave, and do you know what would happen then?

BEN: I'd be very upset, extremely upset, because you'd pulled a gun on me and I'd start driving home, shaking my head, after having come all the way down here, for Christ's sake, *at your request*, you sick prick! And I'd call Julie on the cell phone and tell her that you were delusional. And then she and I would figure out what to do.

JAY: And you might be compelled to call the, uh, authorities and say that there's this guy you know who's talking about etcetera, etcetera. And I would know that that's what you would feel you had to do, and that would mean what? What?

BEN: I don't know.

JAY: Just that I would have to hurry up and proceed with my plan so that I could get it done before the warning would get through.

BEN: So in other words, if I tried to lunge for the phone right now?

JAY: There would be an ugly scene of one kind or another, and you would leave. And your leaving would ensure—would absolutely guarantee—that I would go ahead.

BEN: Oh.

JAY: How is Julie?

BEN: Ummmmm. She's fine, she's doing well, she's good. She's fine.

JAY: And your son, how's he? How old is he now?

BEN: He's thirt—no, that's right, he's fourteen.

JAY: Whoa, fourteen.

BEN: Yep.

JAY: And you've taken up photography.

BEN: Yes.

JAY: It's helpful to have a hobby. I have a hobby, too.

BEN: Jay, assassinating the president isn't a hobby.

JAY: I'm sure not getting paid for it. It's pro bono all the way. So, what are you photographing?

BEN: Oh, I don't want to—nothing—I don't know.

JAY: You must know what you're taking pictures of.

BEN: I'm taking pictures of trees, actually. Tree pictures.

JAY: Trees are good.

BEN: Yes, they're very specific. Each one is different.

JAY: And what are you going to do with these tree pictures?

BEN: They're just for me to have.

JAY: And you've stopped working on your book about the Office of Censorship? What's wrong, man?

BEN: Nothing's wrong.

JAY: Well, then?

BEN: I'm into Cold War territory now.

JAY: What about the Cold War?

BEN: Passive defense.

JAY: Passive defense?

BEN: Yep, that's what I'm looking into. You know what that is?

JAY: No, enlighten me.

BEN: It was the whole idea that we could design things and rearrange things—cities, for instance—so that they would be less damaged during an atomic attack.

JAY: Oh, I see.

BEN: The more spread out the cities are, the harder it is to do a lot of damage with only a few bombs. So there were names for various urban configurations, like the galaxy pattern. I think that was the ideal pattern. One think tank in the sixties did a few studies on "ordered sprawl." That was their dream, ordered sprawl, because it would result in the fewest deaths in a nuclear attack.

JAY: Groovy. And you're looking into this?

BEN: Yeah, and earlier, in the fifties, the tax rules were changed so that developers could use accelerated depreciation when they built strip malls—and so suddenly all these strip malls started making money—and the question is, Why were the rules changed? Was it just the real estate lobby, or was it the civil defense people?

JAY: Oh, I get it.

BEN: And then of course there was the National Defense Highway System—all these ring roads and beltways built to encircle the cities—and what I really want to know is how much institutional overlap was there between the city planners, and the highway planners, and the real estate lobby, and the defense planners?

JAY: Fascinating, very interesting.

BEN: Well, no, it's not that interesting, but it interests me. You go on these little research forays.

JAY: Sure, sure, that's what it's all about. For you.

BEN: Some of the federal money—you may get a kick out of this—some of the money that paid for the studies on ordered sprawl went through the Stanford Research Institute. Now that was a classic Cold War think tank—they were doing all kinds of stuff for the CIA. In fact, the CIA hired them in, I think it was the seventies, to do remote viewing experiments. Did you hear about that?

JAY: No, I don't believe I did.

BEN: Oh, this is your kind of thing. They'd take a psychic—in other words, they'd take some deluded person who thought he was a psychic, or some charlatan pretending to be a psychic—and they'd stick him in a room and give him some map coordinates. And these coordinates were very important, because they corresponded to a location in Russia that the CIA was curious about, where there was a research institute—probably a research institute very similar to the Stanford Research Institute. So the psychic was supposed to sit there and ponder these map coordinates, and tap into the paranormal world, and then he was supposed to draw the buildings that rose up in his mind.

JAY: Psycho-CAD! Nice. Edgy.

BEN: Yep.

JAY: I swear the CIA was a magnet for every drunk and every paranoid wack flake nutjob who'd gotten a college degree.

BEN: It does sometimes seem that way.

JAY: You know, I'm starting to see now that all the totally off-the-wall conspiracy theories, all of them, are true. It's not just that Roosevelt knew about Pearl Harbor. It's not just that Japan was ready to stop fighting before we dropped the bomb. It's that—all right—you've got AIDS developed as part of those germ-warfare experiments in Africa, those monkeys that escaped.

BEN: Jumping species, well, yeah, there's some evidence—

JAY: That's definitely CIA. And then there's the whole thing where we dropped bombs full of bugs and germs on the North Koreans. Another little CIA venture. And the POWs at the time said, Um, yes, we dropped bugs, and an international panel said, Yes, they dropped bugs, and then the professional discreditors went into high gear and came up with that whole rigmarole about "brainwashing," right?—that the POWs who confessed to dropping the bugs must have been subjected to sinister Russian methods of interrogation.

BEN: Mm-hm, I've actually—

JAY: And abstract art! I mean, that was—that was really the last straw for me with the CIA. Abstract painting, promoted by spooks in the federal government to prove how tolerant our democracy is of ugliness. All that awful art, that makes you puke uncontrollably even to be in the same room with it, for all those decades—five long decades—pushed on us by that sorry crew of goofballs at the Central fucking Intelligence Agency!

I mean, it's nuts! It's totally and completely wiggy! And yet it's true.

BEN: I've actually met some of those professional discreditors at conferences. Somebody will present the results of years of painstaking research, careful sifting and weighing of documentary evidence, and these guys pop up and they start tag-teaming: Pish, posh, shoddy research, conspiracy theory, Grassy Knoll, beneath contempt.

JAY: Yeah, well, people really have a desperate need to keep the lid clamped on for as long as possible, because when that kettle blows, and that foulness spews up toward the sky, then we're going to see how rotten it's been in Denmark this whole time. A great and shining nation. It's total tripe, it's forcemeat—it's BAD SAUSAGE, man. We're a bunch of greedy meddlers who don't know the first thing about the countries we're dealing with.

BEN: Generally we know the first thing, but not the second and third.

JAY: Somebody has to be held accountable. Every covert action we've ever engaged in has made the world worse. Every one.

BEN: Are you sure it's every one? Albania, sure.

JAY: Yes, it's every single one. Every shark that

we propped up, every progressive we pushed down. And that's because it's systemic. That's what I'm beginning to recognize. The people who are drawn like moths to covert action, the guys who want to lie and spoof their way through life—they're obviously going to be your sneaks and wackos and paranoids. Or they're depressives who keep trying to lift their mood with higher and higher stakes, like that guy who blew himself away at the top of the stairs.

BEN: Who's that?

JAY: That guy you once told me about.

BEN: You mean Frank Wisner?

JAY: Wisner, yes! So then you have a whole government agency filled to the gills with sneaks and wackos. And the money is flowing like wine. Obviously they're going to screw it up every single time. Look how many years the CIA was in there with the Taliban. Years and years.

BEN: Ah, that was thanks to the Carter administration, that was Zbigniew Brzezinski. Then Reagan and Bush ramped it up hugely. You don't want to think about all that too much, though, because then you get cranky. You want to keep focused, keep to a small canvas.

JAY: Man, I know what you mean about cranky.

I get so cranked up. I mean—so what you're saying basically is that the CIA gave us urban sprawl? Jesus, man, that's—whoo!

BEN: Well, no, no, be careful, now, I wouldn't go that far. There may be some institutional overlaps, that's all I'm saying. But what I'm hoping is that some of the people who did these sprawl studies may still be around, and they may still be sharp enough to shed some light on the fine structure of the events they were part of.

JAY: You want to interview them.

BEN: Yeah, and that's always the painful part of doing Cold War research. You find the number and call, and maybe a son or daughter answers, or maybe a nurse's aide, and then after a long wait your man comes to the phone. He's got a reedy, old-man's voice: "Hello?" He's a guy who once, long ago, had strong, tough feelings toward the Russians, and now he doesn't remember too well what was going on back then, what the motives were, why there was all this bustle and activity. He's probably got pale blue pants on and he's probably not wearing a belt. He's become an outsider in his own life. It seems rude to interview him, and yet—

JAY: And yet you have to, you have to. Don't you? You have to pick up the phone and call him up.

BEN: If you want to tell the story, you at least have to try to talk to him.

JAY: Right. That's right. So you're, ah, sunk pretty darn deep into the fifties and sixties now.

BEN: I am, and I do enjoy learning more and more tiny things—stacking new tidbits onto the tidbits that I've already got stacked. A lot of material was declassified under Clinton. That may be the best thing he did—he didn't like secrecy, except of course in some areas. So yes, I'm still interested in the Second World War, of course, but the fifties lure me as well. But okay, I see where you're going.

JAY: Where am I going? I don't know where I'm going.

BEN: You're wanting to imply that there's equally entrancing material for study right here and now.

JAY: Well—

BEN: And that we can understand it in a fuller way because we're living through it, and that we should be spending time on our time, and not peeling away at these cold, dead onions. That's what you're thinking, isn't it?

JAY: Well, no. Well, sure, yeah. I mean, it is sometimes frustrating to see a person like yourself who is willing to poke and poke into the "fine structure" of stuff that happened back in 1944 or 1954, but who's uninterested in 2004, you know? Here's this whole funky truckload of horror that's going on right now! And yet the digging on the part of the real historians is minimal.

BEN: You try it. Try it with 2004. Be my guest. Blow the lid off it, my man. You'll find it's difficult to do.

JAY: I know it's difficult.

BEN: People are still very much in the middle of their careers, so they're guarded all down the line, and not only is everything classified, but it still feels to them like it needs to be classified, which isn't true about secrets from fifty years ago. And it's so huge, because it's all happening now.

JAY: I know it's huge.

BEN: It's so big that there are no insiders because the inside is all around us. That's the thing. You need a fair amount of condensing and distilling and sheer forgetting to go on before historians like me can get to work.

JAY: Yeah, yeah.

BEN: But that's not the real problem. For me the real problem is that if I worked on Now rather than working on Then I'd have to type these names all the time. Day after day I'd have to be typing "Dennis

Hastert" or "Richard Perle." "Tom DeLay." They're so familiar. They're for journalists. Much more pleasant to type "Stuart Symington" or "Harry Hopkins" or "John Foster Dulles." You see?

JAY: It's an escape.

BEN: Sure it is! Of course it is! I don't want to have to think about William Kristol any more than I have to. That sad sickly smile on TV. I want to think about Herman Kahn. He's dead, he can't do any more harm.

JAY: Who's Herman Kahn?

BEN: Oh, a civil defense nut.

JAY: You could at least map the old onto the new.

BEN: Well, you know, the weird thing about this administration, actually, is that the big guys in it are historical figures already. They've lurched back to life.

JAY: Like Cheney.

BEN: Cheney was part of the Nixon White House; so was Rumsfeld. You can go to the Gerald R. Ford Presidential Library and ask to see the Cheney papers. They're there.

JAY: It's as if these rusted hulks, these zombies, have fought their way back up out of the peat bogs where they've been lying, and they're stumbling around with grubs scurrying in and out of their noses and they're going "We—are—your—advisers."

BEN: Precisely.

JAY: I mean they're there, physically in the White House, making decisions—Dick Cheney! Oh, he's hunched, man, the corruption has completely hunched and gnarled him. His mouth is pulled totally over on one side of his face. It's really—

BEN: And around him are all those freshfaced little Republicans.

JAY: Yes, yes, the applecheeked boys with their cruel mouths, starstruck, I swear they fall in love with these drugstore cowboys. George W. Bush, J. Danforth Quayle. Surrounded by fawners who want to Serve Our Leader. Soon they're going to discover some hormonal thing that leads to right-wing behavior, some very specific deficiency combined with an overdose. You end up mean-spirited, with a high, whiny voice.

BEN: Like Newt.

JAY: Or Orrin Hatch. Or what's his name, Stormin' Norman Schwarzkopf. And the thing I can't figure is, military men seem to want to spend their lives living with other men. Can you make any sense of it? They're out there on some desolate airbase in the middle of nowhere, protecting some future pipeline—eating with other men, shaving with other men. And then actually defecating with other men.

BEN: It's a puzzler.

JAY: Shitting with them, day after day after day! How can they endure it?

BEN: I guess it's like professional football.

JAY: Excuse me for a second, I've got to take a dump.

BEN: Sure.

JAY: No, I'm just kidding.

BEN: Oh, I see.

JAY: And then they stand in the briefing rooms tapping a stick on a map. "These, gentlemen, are our targets of opportunity."

BEN: Yeah, the Democrats—

JAY: And then it begins, the flyovers, and people get hurt. Bombing "campaigns."

BEN: The Democrats do seem more real, somehow. Not all of them. But guys like Barney Frank.

JAY: Barney Frank is great.

BEN: He's articulate, he's funny. I love the guy.

JAY: He's a normal human being.

BEN: Well, and coming from a person such as yourself, that's quite an endorsement.

JAY: Haven't you ever thought about killing somebody? Haven't you?

BEN: Yeah . . . but not. Not. But yeah.

JAY: Okay, then.

BEN: Well, what about Dick Cheney? Are we going to kill him, too?

JAY: We certainly should.

BEN: He's smarter, he's more corrupt, by which I mean he's had more time to capitalize on his corruptions, he's wrecked military procurement—

JAY: But what do you mean, "we"? That's what you said: "Are we going to kill him?"

BEN: Yeah, well, by "we" I mean "you."

JAY: Oh, I see.

BEN: You know, of course, that Cheney tried to block the Freedom of Information Act back when Ford was president? The man is a classic intelligence hack, working to keep everything quiet. There's a nice photograph of him and Rumsfeld together when they were both on staff for Gerald Ford. Rumsfeld's chin was even bigger then.

JAY: Fucking Bobbseys. Cheney was CIA, surely, he has that look.

BEN: Oh, maybe, who knows? Actually, Cheney's first job in Washington was working for Rumsfeld at the Office of Economic Opportunity—Johnson set that up to help poor people. Then Nixon took over and he went, "We'll show those poor people, heh heh," and he put Don Rumsfeld in charge of it. And Rumsfeld kind of got into it. Then later, Rumsfeld and Cheney got extremely rich. Rumsfeld made his bundle when he got the FDA to approve NutraSweet.

JAY: Economic opportunity.

BEN: But no, see, the thing about Cheney is that he's the one. He's the guy who bombed Iraq back in 1991. He and Father Bush tore up those people with cluster bombs, pounded the power stations, the water plants.

JAY: They're responsible.

BEN: The targeting was immoral, and then most of the bombs missed the targets anyways. Sometimes they fell in the sand, sometimes they fell on a house. Not just that one shelter where a hundred cowering civilians died, but over and over.

JAY: And then the years of sanctions.

BEN: Madeleine Albright, God of mercy, that woman! And Clinton goes ahead and does it all over again in Belgrade, with the cluster bombs. Unbelievable. A Rhodes scholar.

JAY: And they know that they're killing innocent people. I remember last year, at the start of this war, that very first day I think it was, General Barry Mc— McArthur?

BEN: McCaffrey.

JAY: General Barry McCaffrey, that *animal*, was on one of the networks as a color commentator, and he himself said, right on network TV, he said, We know we're going to have civilian casualties, because we know that ten percent of the bombs don't go where they're supposed to. It's built in to their statistics.

BEN: Well, in the first Gulf War it wasn't anything like ten percent, because we were getting rid of all those old munitions—sixty percent of the dumb bombs missed, sixty percent. It was a big waste disposal project—the Persian Gulf was the landfill. You dump the expired bombs so that you have to order up fresh new ones. Did you ever by any chance read *Crusade*?

JAY: No, no.

BEN: Well, it's a history of the first Gulf War.

There's a moment in there—it's by a guy who writes for the *Post*, and he interviewed a ton of people— there's a moment in there that sums up the whole war, the futility of it.

JAY: What is it?

BEN: This battleship is stationed somewhere off the coast of Kuwait. So it shells the coast and it shells the coast, and then the assessment people fly over and they say, Okay, you're done, you've totally destroyed everything that needs to be destroyed, mission accomplished, you can stop your shelling now, nice job. And the captain of the ship goes to somebody, I think he went to Schwarzkopf, and he says, "General, my ship is due for scrapping. This is its last moment of glory. When we go home all the old shells we have on board will have to be decommissioned, and that'll be very expensive. So what do you say?" And so Schwarzkopf, or whoever it is, goes, "Okay, sure." And so the ship sits in the water lobbing more shells into Kuwait, blowing up stuff that's already been blown up fifty times over.

JAY: Waste disposal.

BEN: That's it, that's what it was, when it wasn't simple savagery. That was the war that really undid me. Seeing those bombs float down silently on TV. My blood froze, I had to turn everything off—I remember one night I went down to the basement and I sat there for ten minutes listening to the furnace. All those sorties, and Morton Kondracke and Fred Barnes on TV cheerfully chatting away.

JAY: They were high on it.

BEN: Suddenly everyone was using that word, "sorties." We'd been working with Saddam for years. Total devastation. That's on Dick Cheney's head, and George Senior's head. Not George W.'s head. He was just fooling around with a baseball team back then.

JAY: They got away with it in '91.

BEN: They got away with it.

JAY: This time, they won't.

BEN: Well, we'll see. Who knows whether the man will be reelected or not? At the moment, he's dropping, but he may bounce back.

JAY: He won't be reelected, because he's going to be dead. Marines standing in rows with their hands on their hearts, hundreds of limousines, mourners filing past.

BEN: Come off it.

JAY: No, this time, this war, that he imposed on the world, when the whole world said no to him so CLEARLY, in the streets, in every country, this war that he forced on humanity—this war will be avenged!

BEN: Okay, but first, how about we get a bite to eat? I'm ready to chew my thumb off. I drove all the way down here at eighty miles an hour because I thought you were going to jump out a window.

JAY: The window does open.

BEN: That's nice to know. Listen, I saw a couple of restaurants on the way in. We could go, or I could—I could just, you know, I could hop out for a second and get us something and be back in a jiffy.

JAY: No, no, no, no need to do that. You might come back with federal agents, and we need to continue this. There's room service.

BEN: That'll work.

JAY: And the menu's here somewhere. Ah: "All Day Dining." Club sandwiches. Hey, I can tell you they make a peppercorn steak that's kind of nice. I had it last night.

BEN: Have they got a Caesar salad?

JAY: They do. You want that?

BEN: Yes, I would. A Caesar salad and a steak.

JAY: Good.

BEN: On me, though.

JAY: No, you drove all the way down.

BEN: No, no, no. You said you're having pecuniary difficulties.

JAY: Yeah, but that's not really going to matter too much. I'm charging everything to my room. *Hi—yes, is this Inez? Hi, Inez. I talked to you last night, I believe. How are you? Good. We'd like to order some lunch. That's right. For two. My friend's in town. Ben. Could we possibly have, let's see, one Caesar salad. . . .* You want anchovies on that?

BEN: Sure.

JAY: *That's an enthusiastic yes to the anchovies. And the peppercorn steak, please. It was so good last night.* How do you want it cooked?

BEN: Medium.

JAY: *He'd like it very well done, please.*

BEN: No no.

JAY: It's okay. *And a cheeseburger and fries. Extremely well done. Right. And we'll have a big bottle of, uh, sparkling water. Not flavored, just clean, fresh sparkling water. That's it. And a big tub of coffee, as well. That'll be great. Thanks, take it easy.* Boy, she's very nice. She says half an hour. We can have some bagel chips or something now from the minibar if you want.

BEN: No, I'll just wait for my, uh, very well done steak.

JAY: You have to do that these days, trust me. If you say you want it medium, they'll bring it to you raw, and I mean raw raw, bleeding all over the plate. Just raw.

BEN: I see, so if you ask for well done—

JAY: If you ask for well done, you get medium rare. I've been there, man. If you ask for very well done, you get medium. And that's what you wanted.

BEN: How do you get well done?

JAY: There's no way, it's impossible. Nobody's going to cook your steak well done in this day and age. Forget it.

BEN: Well, thanks for looking out for me.

JAY: No problem. Yee, it's bright out. Let's crack the window a little.

BEN: Why?

JAY: Just to be aware of what's going on outside. Way over there, beyond those trees, that's where the snipers are on the roof. The sharpshooters. But that's okay, because I've got my special bullets.

BEN: Consider this: You kill him and *boing*, Cheney's driving the truck. He's twice as bad.

JAY: Well, once you go down that road, man— that's a slippery slope, let me tell you. You start to think, Okay, I know I've got to get rid of Bush, oh,

49

but wait, Cheney's twice as bad, got to take him out, too, maybe some kind of tiny scorpion that climbs up his leg just as he's being sworn in, bites him, he slumps. The scorpion has no memory of what it's done—*The Manchurian Scorpion*. But wait, hmm, Rumsfeld's just as bad as Cheney, so in fairness—and don't forget Powell—maybe you don't kill Powell, because he was less enthusiastic, maybe you just want to put him in a coma. And then there's Tommy Franks and General Richard Myers, with all his medals, and it just goes on and on. And eventually you start thinking you have to somehow do away with about thirty or forty people. Which is pretty outrageous. And then you think, well, thirty or forty people, what's that? That's NOTHING. They've killed thousands of innocent people. People who are utterly blameless. Thousands of people who have nothing whatsoever to do with any warlike activity.

BEN: Yeah, no, wrong road, we definitely don't want to go down that road.

JAY: The proportions are skewed. It's like peeking into the hole in one of those miniature rooms—those little Dr. Caligari rooms, where everything looks right, but it isn't right at all. People think these prison photos prove how bad the war is.

Actually, no, the prison photos are nice compared with how bad the war is. If the prisoners had had clothes on, even bloody clothes, the Republicans would have said, Hey, sometimes you have to break a few eggs, you know. It's the nakedness that made it a scandal.

BEN: Perhaps so.

JAY: They say, in hushed tones, they say, "Some of the Prisoners Have Died." Well, what the fuck? Yes, some have died. Some have been packed in ice and spirited away. But more than ten thousand Iraqis have been killed in this war. It's off the charts. Tanks firing on apartment blocks. Morgues and hospitals filled to capacity, blood splashed on the walls. None of it is secret. It's known, it's been reported around the world for a full year, and yet there's no outrage about that, there's no scandal. What, that? Oh, that's just the war. I mean, standing naked with a hood over your head while a dog barks at your dick, okay, that's horrible, but having a missile hit your house is a hell of a lot worse, because you may be carrying your own kid out of the rubble.

BEN: There's something really sinister about those hoods.

JAY: The hoods are bad, it's all bad! It's so

unbelievably bad! How can somebody like Wolfowitz be involved in this? That quiet delivery that he has. He's certainly smarter than Bush—I'd even say he's smarter than Rumsfeld.

BEN: Julie says he must have been persecuted when he was a kid, one of those playground victims. He was in on the first Gulf War, you know. He was there urging Cheney on, right from the beginning.

JAY: Was he?

BEN: Yeah, he was so unhappy when we didn't go in, when we stopped at the gates of the city. Now he's got his wish.

JAY: I want to talk to him, I want to reason with him, I want to say, "Wolfowitz, you fuckhead! You're killing people! You're not humble enough before the mystery of a foreign country!"

BEN: Somehow I don't think you'd get very far.

JAY: But I don't want to send my scorpion after him. That's the thing. I don't feel he has to die. He should be one of those guys who go to jail for a while, and they grow a beard because they're tired of seeing their face in the news.

BEN: They write their memoirs, like John Ehrlichman.

JAY: Yeah, I think Wolfowitz is genuinely crazy,

but in a stealthy way, so you don't pick up on it at first. Whereas, as you know, people think I'm a little off, but really I'm on an even keel. I'm just candid. I mean, sure there have been some problems—but I'm steady!

BEN: You're a bit ragged around the edges, that's all. What was I going to ask you, though? Oh, yeah. Have you ever been fingerprinted?

JAY: Yes, I have.

BEN: And have you . . . talked to anybody else about this?

JAY: Not in so many words.

BEN: Nobody?

JAY: I may have used the word "assassination" once or twice, but not with any specifics.

BEN: What happened with that nice woman you were going with?

JAY: Which one was that?

BEN: That one I met? Sarah, was it? Lots of bracelets?

JAY: Oh, Sarah.

BEN: She was very nice.

JAY: She moved on to other things. I ranted and raved too much.

BEN: Ah. Do you ever see Lila? How about your kids?

JAY: Sure, yeah.

BEN: And how are they?

JAY: It's a little hard to tell. The youngest and the oldest are into their own little worlds, but Mara's twelve now, and she's got some real fire in her. Maybe she'll carry the torch when I'm gone. It's hard to say good-bye to them. But I did. Sometimes you've got say, Okay, this is my thing, and I am going to do it. Nobody else can do it.

BEN: I really don't think this is your thing.

JAY: I just wore Lila out. You know? With me, everything's political. I mean, she's political, too, but not as much. A couple of years ago I got into a spat with her father. He's one of those people who's simply not capable of rational thought. So it was a little unpleasant. And the children weren't in the room but they were in the other room. All of that led to a word of wisdom from the judge, that I should moderate my behavior. And that affected how much I see the kids. I've made a bollix of my life, that's for sure.

BEN: You mean you've bollixed it up?

JAY: Yes, I bollixed it up!

BEN: Well, shouldn't you try to un-bollix it? Why would you think that doing this would help in any way?

JAY: You know that sounds very therapeutic, and I don't want you to be therapeutic. I just want you to be an attentive person I can talk to.

BEN: Yeah, but see, what you're doing here, though, and I say this as gently as I can, is you're using me. I didn't know when you called that you wanted to tape our discussion prior to killing the president of the United States. I did not know that. If I had known that I would have said, No thank you, I'm going to be scanning some transparencies and I think you better call somebody else, because I'm not going to drive to Washington to hear the gory details.

JAY: I know, you wouldn't have come.

BEN: What you said was "I really need to talk to you." And I thought, Oh, okay, he really needs to talk to me. Sounds like the poor guy is in a crisis state. We've all been in states of despair. But, but. I didn't know that you wanted to talk to me about doing *this*. I don't like this. And then, this whole thing that you just laid on me, that if I call the law you're going to whip out a firearm and all that—I don't like it. I'm not sure that I want to be threatened with violence, with being shot in the leg, it's not enjoyable. I'm not going to tolerate it, in fact. I'm going to walk out right now.

JAY: Go ahead. You threatened me first with John Ashcroft, you know. But go. Go.

BEN: If I walk out right now, are you going to go off and do something absurd and permanent and horrible, and something that's going to totally unhinge the world even more than it is unhinged? Are you going to cause bloodshed?

JAY: I'm going to prevent a certain amount of bloodshed. By causing a minor blip of bloodshed in one human being I'm going to prevent further bloodshed.

BEN: But that's where you're completely misguided. And I'm your friend, I can say this to you. You're completely misguided in that. It could cause any amount of bloodshed. If you think— what's your plan? Okay, first of all—let's see the gun.

JAY: I may have one.

BEN: You said that. I want to see it.

JAY: You want to see some bullets? They're special bullets.

BEN: All right, show me the special bullets.

JAY: First I need to know whether you're in or out.

BEN: What? I'm out, I'm so out.

JAY: Are you with me or not?

BEN: I'm not with you! Not with you.

JAY: I'm disappointed but I can't say that I'm surprised.

BEN: I don't mean to hurt your feelings, Jay. But I don't even want to impeach the guy. He's committed impeachable offenses—lied us into a war.

JAY: That war speech he gave on the eve of the attack—he was bonkers that night. Staring. "When the dictator has departed . . ."

BEN: Well, so—should he be impeached? My feeling is that maybe he should be, if you consider his case in isolation. But you can't do that. If we now impeach him after that whole rigmarole with Clinton, then we're on this nightmare seesaw where each side tries to impeach the other side and the country goes even further down the toilet.

JAY: Imagine if somebody had the sense to kill him last year, during that speech. Imagine if somebody had wired up the leads from an eleciric chair to the podium. So he walks up, he lays out his papers, he takes hold of both sides of the podium in that authoritative way, and *buzzap*. Imagine how much death the world would have been spared. All that looting. The antiquities.

BEN: I think the war machine would have ground on.

JAY: Oh, no, no, I can't agree. It would definitely have slowed things up. No question. Do you want to see the bullets?

BEN: You know what you need?

JAY: What?

BEN: A dog. A puppy.

JAY: Well, I travel a lot, so I don't think I could have a puppy. It would be nice. I worked for a roofer in Birmingham for a while, he was a Korean guy, really smart, his eyes had been burned by the sun, he never wore sunglasses. It gets so hot up there on those houses, wow, really hot. You can't touch anything, everything's glittering. It's a hostile environment. One guy fell and cracked a rib. But then he was right back up there. I think that job sautéed my brain.

BEN: It's possible.

JAY: Something was readjusted, anyway.

BEN: Recalibrated, eh? As Rumsfeld would say?

JAY: Recalibrated. I got a new perspective. I feel I want my life to count for something.

BEN: Lots of people feel that.

JAY: I feel it more intensely now. But no, I

definitely couldn't have had a puppy because I was gone all day.

BEN: I guess not.

JAY: One of the roofers was a kind of interesting guy who was trying to raise free-range chickens. Before work he'd drive out to some land and get all his chickens going. He had this enclosure that he moved around on the land, so that the chickens would have a new patch of grass to mess around in, and I gave some thought to starting a chicken farm, but the guy said that it wasn't really accurate to call it free-range, because the kind of chicken that customers expect, that restaurants expect, is a super, super fleshy chicken, it's a kind of monster, and when a chicken puts on that much flesh, it can't walk very well, so that even though it has more room to peck in than a factory chicken that's been, you know, raised in solitary confinement, still it's been bred for meat for so many generations that it's really more or less imprisoned by its own bulk. One day we were having a drink and he was all upset because one of his birds had gotten its leg crushed under the frame when he was moving it that morning, so he had to slaughter it.

BEN: That's unfortunate.

JAY: Yeah, he invited me over to his place and we ate the chicken. Kind of a wistful moment.

BEN: How was it?

JAY: The chicken? It was good. It might have tasted a little more content with its lot, hard to say. After a while, though, I couldn't take being on a roof all day long, and the chicken man told me about a fisherman up near Cape Cod who needed some help. So I went up there for a few months and hauled lobster pots. Now *that* is work, that is punishing work.

BEN: I bet.

JAY: Your arms, your back, oh. But I need to be tired at the end of the day, physically exhausted. I don't want any free time in the middle of the afternoon, because then I start brooding on political stuff and also that's when I start wanting a sip of something. Amber waves of grain, know what I mean?

BEN: I know.

JAY: I couldn't have had a puppy then, either.

BEN: Nope, not if you're out on a boat all day.

JAY: Nope, no puppy. No possible puppy.

BEN: . . . So where are the bullets, Jay?

JAY: They're in the, um—I don't know if I want to tell you. I'm not sure you're fully committed.

BEN: I'm not committed. I would like to disarm you.

JAY: I'm on a path, man.

BEN: Well, veer off it.

JAY: There will be no veering. We've lost every war we've fought. Winning is losing. We lost the Second World War.

BEN: I think it's widely agreed that we won World War II.

JAY: Well, we didn't. It was the beginning of the end.

BEN: In what way?

JAY: We bombed all those places—we bombed Japan, right down the islands, cities turned into grave sites. The crime of it began to work on us afterward, it began chewing on our spleens and rotting us out inside.

BEN: Ugh.

JAY: The guilt of it squeezed us and it twisted us and made us need to keep more and more things secret that shouldn't have been kept secret. We tried to pretend that we were good midwestern folks, eating our church suppers—that we'd done the right thing over there. But it was so completely, shittingly false.

BEN: Yes, in a sense, but—

JAY: And so we lost that war. We didn't win it. We were corrupted by it, and we became more and more warlike and secretive, and we spent all our money building weaponry and subverting little governments, poking here and there and propping up loathsome people, United Fruit. And the gangrene spread through the whole loaf of cheese.

BEN: Oh, please.

JAY: And Japan couldn't do that. Their best people spent their days and nights thinking about how to make beautiful things, tools, machines that just felt good to hold. Which they did with such artistry. They couldn't make fighter planes, we didn't let them. And so they won the war. We lost.

BEN: Okay, listen, where's your gun, dammit? Where is it?

JAY: I can let you see the bullets. They're in with a picture in a biscuit tin.

BEN: Where are they?

JAY: Top drawer. Under the TV.

BEN: I don't see any.

JAY: In the back.

BEN: In here? Whoa! There really are bullets here.

JAY: I told you there were. They're specials.

BEN: What's special about them?

JAY: Okay, the bullets are self-guided. They're programmable. I'm almost finished programming them. They're marinating.

BEN: They just look like normal bullets to me.

JAY: Appearances can be deceiving.

BEN: Where'd you get them?

JAY: I'll take them. Hand them over. Thanks. I got them through a guy.

BEN: What guy?

JAY: Just a guy I talked to.

BEN: Yeah?

JAY: Yeah, I'd heard from the guy who made the, uh, remote-controlled CD saws that there was a man in Cleveland who had these homing bullets, and all you had to do was put the bullets in a box along with a photograph of the person you wanted to shoot and they were able to seek that person out and—and that's it.

BEN: So what did you do, did you just ring his doorbell and say, Hello, I'd like to buy some of your bullets?

JAY: No, I called him up and I said in a casual way that I'd heard that some particularly accurate bullets might be available. And he said, You mean you want the specials? And I said yeah. And he said,

**63**

Okay, fifty dollars apiece. He overnighted them
to me.

BEN: So, did he ask you what you were going to
do with them?

JAY: He did. I said I wanted them because of the
checkpoint. And he said, Think about it before you
do it. And I said I would. And I paced around. All
yesterday afternoon I paced and I walked, and I
went to the natural history museum, I bought a
natural history hat there, you like it?

BEN: Yeah, it's a nice hat. Very practical.

JAY: And I wondered what this city would look
like after I did it. How would the city look with this
man gone? And I realized that the city would not
look very different at all. You know? It isn't like air-
to-ground missiles from an A-10 Warthog ripping
into a neighborhood. A small, violent point would
have been pressed home, that's all. But I also
realized, of course, that I would probably be arrested
and executed, or just shot, and therefore I wanted
some record of what I'd done and why I did it. So I
called you.

BEN: There are six bullets here.

JAY: Well, they're not foolproof. But if he's
within range, all I have to do is point the gun in
more or less the right direction, and the bullet does

the rest. It's like one of those precision guided missiles, Lockheed missiles, except with built-in face recognition.

BEN: A Bush-seeking bullet.

JAY: That's right.

BEN: Agh! I have a family. I have a wife, I have a son. I have a job. This is so crazy.

JAY: I'm sorry, Ben, for involving you in this— endeavor.

BEN: If the FBI and the Secret Service and what's his name, Tom Ridge, come after me because I've been hanging out with you in a hotel room before you make some crazy attempt on the life of the president, I'm totally cooked. I'm totally cooked, all right? I'll have to say, Well, what we were talking about was—you know. What am I going to do, lie? I can't lie. You and I sat here talking about the pros and cons of—of— Yes, you were talking a lot of delusional gobblydegook about homing bullets, but basically your intent was clear. I'll have to say that. I'm scared. We're both going to Guantánamo Bay.

JAY: Gitmo, hell—we're going to Abu Ghraib. They'll put us in the cages, we'll be up on the stools. We're dead men.

BEN: I don't want to be a dead man.

JAY: Oh, stop fretting. You can say, which is quite

true, that you argued against it. And that, however—you weren't sure—but you felt that you'd perhaps succeeded in convincing me not to go ahead with it.

BEN: Perhaps succeeded, okay, good, okay.

JAY: In fact, if you'd like I can just tell you right now, I can just say, you did convince me. I'm not going to take the gun and go do it, because you were just so damn compelling in making a case that the president should be allowed to live, because, you know, he's a bad guy but, you know, killing is wrong, and it's not a good thing to do, and it's pretty darn bad, and blah blah. You know? You did it. You did a marvelous job of dissuading me.

BEN: You fff— Oh, I'm not happy.

JAY: You just need some lunch. And a drink.

BEN: You know, this isn't frivolity.

JAY: I'm not being frivolous. There is zero frivolity in my outlook right now. It's time. It's way past time. All you have to do is spend a couple of hours on a computer looking up stuff. Look at the pictures of the dead and injured. I did it last night.

BEN: You have a computer here?

JAY: I used the business center downstairs. Look at the pictures. It hurts bad. But do it. There was a child with a severely burned face. And then—are you listening to me? Then, go look at Lockheed Martin's website. Read their press releases. They make the missiles that deliver the cluster bombs that destroyed those people. And then think for just a moment about the fact that Lynne Cheney was on the board of directors of Lockheed. She was. Right up until when her husband became vice president. Lockheed! The vileness of what they do. It fucking buggers understanding. I printed—

BEN: "Buggers" or "beggars"?

JAY: Take your pick. I printed out one of their web pages, where is it? Yeah, here. Here. Lockheed Martin Aeronautics. It says that their products "help ensure peace and stability around the world." Have you ever in your life heard anything more patently false than that?

BEN: That's a little over the top, I must say.

JAY: Fort Worth, Texas, is where they make the F-16, the killer plane. There's all this tough talk of "lethality" and "extreme lethality." They sell these weapons and warplanes all over, and the countries that buy them, like Turkey, buy them with aid money from the United States. So in other words, we pay other countries to buy these machines from

Lockheed. Holy mackerel-economics! Cheney's wife was on the board of directors of Lockheed from something like 1994 to 2001. She was getting a hundred and twenty thousand a year for helping to guide and oversee this merchant of misery. Lynne Cheney, this merchant of multinational MISERY, man. It's staggering when you take time to think about it for more than twelve seconds. And here she's all in a flusterment about the nasty lyrics of Eminem.

BEN: Eminem is no favorite of mine.

JAY: Well, no, he's not Zappa. But that woman, I'm sorry to say, is the real obscenity.

BEN: Oh, Lynne Cheney did some good things when she was at the NEH. You've got to lighten up a little. She's not a viper. She was just on the board of directors.

JAY: How could she be on the board of that company and look at herself in the mirror? How can she look at her husband in the mirror? Halliburton and Enron and all that. Enron wangling to profit from the pipeline across Afghanistan. It's a sickening spectacle.

BEN: Do you think they look at each other in the mirror?

JAY: Probably they do from time to time. But

you know, the straightforward corruption is never worth wasting too much time over. There are always going to be corrupt people who sip from the firehose. No, it's the death-dealing. It's the creation of suffering and hate. That's when you have to move.

BEN: Yeah, yeah, okay, but—yeah, all right, all right, this is all relevant and useful information. Dick Cheney is the shadow warrior—it does certainly seem that way. And Lynne Cheney was until very recently in the pay of the arms merchants. But that's just the Cheneys. And you're talking about—

JAY: I'm talking about direct action against the guy who's nominally in charge. George W. Tumblewad. If you as the guy in charge allow killing to go forward, if you in fact actively promote killing, if you order it to happen—if you say, Go, men, launch the planes, start the bombing, shock and awe the living crap out of that ancient city—you are going to create assassins like me. That's the basic point I'm making. You are going to create the mad dogs that will maul you. And that's what he's done.

BEN: Oh, Jay. My head, my head. I have a job. Let me have those bagel chips, will you? Oh, man. So, I take it, um, you're no longer in the lobster business?

JAY: I had to bring that effort to a close.

BEN: Why? Seems like the fresh air, you know.

JAY: I saw one too many lobsters. They're primitive creatures, extremely primitive. What goes on in those cold heads down in the murk at the bottom of the bay? Some people get terrified looking up at the emptiness of the night sky. I get that exact sensation looking at a lobster.

BEN: So you've been between positions?

JAY: Well, no, I've been working for a landscaping company in Tennessee, moving flagstones around, stone benches. For a while I had this idea that I wanted to get a job in a real factory, so that I could be part of something important, some manufactured product that went all over the country and went into everyone's life, I wanted to punch a clock, *whomp*, time to work, just do the same thing over and over, go into autopilot, and that's when I started to get a troubled feeling.

BEN: A troubled feeling, you? Hah hah hah! Who would have thought!

JAY: I still had this childish image of a factory in my head, which is obviously no longer a true idea, because face it, we're not making anything anymore. It's kind of scary.

BEN: Well—

JAY: What do we make? Huh? Do we make TVs, do we make shoes, do we make pillowcases, do we make electric motors? Do we make radios? Clocks? Dishes? Forks? Knives? What do we make? Hammers?

BEN: We make pickup trucks.

JAY: That's for sure. We make light trucks for fascist fiddlefucks to drive around in.

BEN: We make corn syrup.

JAY: Corn syrup. That we do.

BEN: Military hardware?

JAY: There you go. Unmanned CIA robot attack drones. We do make those. Although I bet if we could we'd be outsourcing our attack drones to the Chinese. Slap an FAA sticker on them and sell them to tiny fearful countries.

BEN: The Chinese-made attack drones would probably be more reliable. Cheaper, too . . . What? What? What is it?

JAY: Oh, just remembering. Three men are standing on a bombed-out hillside in the mountains in Afghanistan. Do you recall that episode? They're loading up a camel with some shrapnel that they've gathered to sell for scrap across the border in Pakistan. They're scavengers. Finally here's something American that actually helps them survive—the bomb shrapnel itself. A gift from the skies. And then a Predator attack drone flies by, *rmmmmmmmmmmmmmmm*, very slow, *rmmmmmmmmmmm*, odd-looking plane, headless, and its camera gets a fix on them, and it turns, *rmmmmmmmmmmmmm*, and some CIA drone jockey sitting in front of a screen sipping lemonade thinks, Woo Nelly, tall guys, long beards, robes—robes? ROBE ALERT, ROBE ALERT, ROBE ALERT, one Adam-Twelve, men wandering on the hills near the caves! Al Qaeda operatives! Could be Mr. Bin himself! So the CIA guy takes another sip of lemonade, pushes a few buttons, and suddenly the three men see this flare of a Hellfire missile, they hear the hiss of it, and they pause, and for some curious reason it's coming toward them, it curves a little, it seems to know where they are, and boom, shreds of blood and tissue, moaning people. I knew, I knew when those towers came down, I knew we would be bombing somewhere very soon. It's what we do. We get as far away as we possibly can and then we deliver the goods.

BEN: Does Lockheed make those Predators?

JAY: No, somebody else does that. They make the Hellfire missile, though. I do know that. And I'll tell you something else. Lockheed has a joint venture with Israel's state weapons company, Rafael. It's called P-G-S-U-S, Precision Guided Something Something United States. PGSUS. Israel supposedly makes forty-five percent of this missile and Lockheed makes fifty-five percent of it. That way it can be deemed a U.S. product and not an Israeli product. It's called the Popeye II missile. Any chips left?

BEN: Finish the bag.

JAY: So here we are in an attack on Arab cities shooting Israeli-designed missiles at them. And so lo and behold then you've got people in robes in Baghdad who are holding up bits of bombs that say "Made in Jerusalem." I mean, that's a guarantee, that's an iron-clad guarantee that you're going to have decades of smoldering hate. Terrorism out the wing-wang. I mean, damn! We can't even make our own missiles anymore. I'm going to kill him. No shit. Four billion a month we're spending for this war.

BEN: Yeah, can you imagine the rail network we could build with that?

JAY: I'm telling you, he's one dead armadillo.

BEN: We still make antidepressants. That's a

cheery spot on the horizon. The pharmaceutical industry. Don Rumsfeld's old stomping ground.

JAY: Pills, pickup trucks, and war, that's it.

BEN: That's not really it.

JAY: That's really it.

BEN: No, actually, seriously, we do still make balsa airplanes. I like those.

JAY: That's something. But yesterday I was shaving and I thought, Hey, do we make any lightbulbs in this country anymore? I kind of shivered for a second. It was like a cat walking over the country's grave.

BEN: Well, do we?

JAY: I don't think we do. I know that General Electric bulbs are made in Mexico and Canada, because I always check, I check everything now, it's one of the few good laws left, that a product has to proclaim its origin. And you really have to hand it to those Chinese, I mean part of it is extreme poverty and slave labor, but you're right, a lot of it is that they're willing to do careful work all day long, fine sustained work, assembling little parts, painting little patterns, painting those molded dogs, the buildings in the snowy paperweights. And the Happy Meal toys.

BEN: Yeah, those are—

JAY: Bart Simpson on a skateboard and you look closely at him and there'll be eight colors painted on this thing with a very very precise brush, and then, the tiny letters molded underneath, CHINA.

BEN: Or PRC, People's Republic of China—I've seen that.

JAY: We're living in this time of superabundance where's it's like there are a billion Geppettos and they're all doing this masterful work and it's just being given away, it's not even valued properly, You want a toy? Here, take it, it's worthless, finish your fries. The stuff coming from India now, beautiful inlay, kids are doing it, and meanwhile we can't even make an exhaust pipe anymore.

BEN: Yeah, but I bet you this country could reindustrialize itself very fast. We could do it in five years if we had to. Well, ten years.

JAY: I'm not sure we'll ever get it back. We're at the end. You know what the biggest employer is?

BEN: In the U.S., you mean? The military. I think it's over a million people. Heavily indoctrinated, mostly Republican.

JAY: Well, okay, after that.

BEN: I'd say, hmm, the road-paving industry.

Every little town has its team of road pavers. I'd say it's asphalt manufacturing, and parking lots and roads and highways.

JAY: Well, but what company, what single corporation?

BEN: Oh, you mean Wal-Mart?

JAY: Yes of course I mean Wal-Mart. Here's a company whose mission is to buy stuff really cheap from other countries and put it on shelves here in the ugliest architectural environment you could ever imagine, that blue and that gray, big American flags hanging from the ceiling—and the light, God, that shadowless scary light that fills the place, acres of that pitiless light. "I confess, I shot the sheriff, please, take the light away!"

BEN: I'll tell you, my son has always loved going to Wal-Mart. On our last trip there I bought a DVD of the *Andy Griffith Show*. It cost five dollars and fifty cents. We got a delicious pretzel on the way out. And there were friendly chatty women in the crafts and sewing area.

JAY: What were they chatting about?

BEN: Who was going to go on break first.

JAY: Anyway, it's pretty dang ugly.

BEN: I'll concede that. But then, if you're going to talk retailing, there's Old Navy. The old truck in the middle of the store with all the T-shirts heaped around it?

JAY: Old Navy's good. Target's good.

BEN: And the shop windows in New York City— we can be proud of those, can't we? I mean, are you really trying to tell me that you're going to kill George W. Bush because Wal-Mart is ugly?

JAY: It's a contributing factor, it really is.

BEN: That's just plain screwy.

JAY: Sam Walton's kids are some of the richest people in the world. The money those four have, twenty billion dollars apiece—it's enough to make you shit. It's like they're sitting in tiny rubber dinghies, floating on seas of hog waste. And it all came from those stores. Our country's dying, man! We're killing people and we're dying at the same time! I brought a hammer along.

BEN: Oh, boy.

JAY: It's a basic tool. Remember What's-Her-Name who gave her husband forty whacks? The man deserves a good bludgeoning.

BEN: Stop it, Jay. That's brutal. Why do you keep singling him out? We've had bad presidents for fifty years.

JAY: He's the absolute worst. He's the broken pickle.

BEN: The broken pickle?

JAY: The one at the bottom of the jar, with the seeds swirling around it.

BEN: You're looking for someone to blame. Everyone does this. I do it. I could feel myself doing it this morning when I was driving down here. I went past about four Staples and two BJ's Wholesale Clubs and a Fuddruckers and a couple Wal-Marts and a Circuit City and a this and a that—all these cars going in both directions—and as usual I began to think, Why the heck is anyone bothering to drive anywhere in this country? Wherever you go, it's the same.

JAY: It's terrifying, isn't it? Some places are hotter, some places more people speak Spanish, that's about it. Nothing's local, we're nowhere!

BEN: Right, it's the triumph of the galaxy pattern. So I start thinking, What was the demonic force that did this to us? What cabal was it? Who can I blame? You say, Oho, the Republicans. Aha, the president. I go, Oh ho ho, it was those cold warriors of yore, those passive defense think-tankers, who did this to us, who destroyed our cities, but the truth is—

JAY: Hang on a second. *Hi, Inez, just checking on our lunch. Great, thanks.*

BEN: Is it on its way?

JAY: Shouldn't be long.

BEN: Okay, but the truth is we did it ourselves. We thought we wanted it this way. Most people like driving around all day. None of this was the result of George W.—it's the result of millions of tiny individual decisions.

JAY: Yeah, but sometimes you reach a point where you realize that millions of tiny individual decisions are condensed into one man. That's what I'm up against.

BEN: I'm telling you, they were all bad. Honestly. Truman, Eisenhower, both bad. Kennedy? Devious, totally unfaithful. All he had was a smile. "Ask not," my ass, he was no good. Kennedy, then Johnson, Johnson was no good. Nixon, no good. Bad. Lousy. Ford? No good. Carter? Meant well, no good. Reagan: terrible. Bush Senior, worse. Very bad. Horrible. Mired us in military debt. Filled the government with intelligence agents. Disgusting, disgusting, loathsome, horrible. And a whiner, too. Godawful man. Who else? Ah, then we had Clinton. What's the first thing he does when he gets into office? He sends planes into Iraq, some "sorties," just to show he's no slacker.

JAY: Kills people.

BEN: Lost me right there. Later on he and Wesley Clark bomb Belgrade. They bomb the TV station!

JAY: And kill more people.

BEN: Clinton, bad. And now we have George W. Bush. Really bad. Hellacious. Stole the election, etcetera. So you're going to single out this one guy? Of all these people, one of them was killed in office. You're going to make it that two of these mediocrities were killed in office?

JAY: Yes.

BEN: Well, I'm sorry. We are so close to financial collapse in this country. We're just on the edge. We're hollow. The termites have been munching for decades. Then you come along and cause a crisis.

JAY: Exactly!

BEN: Great, now we've got true panic. Asian countries don't want our debt. We have no cash, no credit, nothing to sell except weapons. We're a bankrupt, bankrupt country. Our consumer industries are prescription drugs and corn sweetener. What's going to happen when all that comes out? If it comes out gradually, maybe the world can adjust. Maybe there won't be looting. Holland was a world power once. Maybe we'll end up humble, like the Dutch are, and regroup. If it comes out suddenly, though, maybe there will be a collapse. Who suffers then? The poor suffer. Maybe we end up with several regional territories run by Samoan strongmen. Who knows? I don't know. It's all going to come out eventually no matter what happens to any president, but I sure think it'll be a lot better all around if it comes out at a trickle.

JAY: No, it's much simpler than that. The guy can't be allowed to get away with murder. Period. The government shouldn't execute him, because the government shouldn't be in the business of taking people's lives. It has to be an individual. Which is me. If what I do causes an upheaval, okeydoke. The sooner we get our comeuppance, the sooner we stop being a world bully, and the sooner the dying stops. You know what's totally fucked us up? Morally?

BEN: What?

JAY: Abortion.

BEN: Ugh. Don't you have enough to think about?

JAY: No, this is very much a part of it, because I think one reason this country is so totally messed up and in the viselike grip of these brownshirts and these radio wackos right now is because the left decided, Okay, here's our big issue, "reproductive rights." Well, it's not a good issue at all, and it introduced an inconsistency into the liberal position, a huge inconsistency that the right then exploited, and will continue to exploit until the left is destroyed. If the Democrats weren't so bullheadedly pro-abortion we wouldn't be in Iraq now.

BEN: How's that?

JAY: Because Bush wouldn't have won. Bush won because gentle-hearted people heard the fakery, the falsehood. "Pro-choice." It's audible.

BEN: So what's your position? Make it illegal?

JAY: It's illegal already. I mean, if it's a couple thousand cells, the size of an aphid, well, fine. Ladybug, okay. Water strider? Hmmmm. But then very quickly we're talking about something the size of a mouse, and that's important. The size of a mouse. A mammal. Then our protective instincts come into play and our instincts say, Hey, this is a vulnerable innocent creature and we can't just suck it out of its burrow and let it die there on a steel tray. It should be protected under the laws of the country.

BEN: What's the law now? I have to tell you I don't think about this much. I avoid it.

JAY: The law now is basically that you can have an abortion if the baby would die if it was born.

BEN: I see.

JAY: And the pro-choice fact sheets say things like eighty percent of abortions are performed when the fetus is less than two and a half inches long. That's about the size of the Indian in the Cupboard. Why would we think that because it's two inches long we can kill it? Dr. Seuss knew what he was talking about.

BEN: What do you mean?

JAY: "A person's a person, no matter how small."

BEN: God, I bet you're popular at parties.

JAY: The right wing is right on this, I'm telling you. This is murder. It is. You don't have to be a Christian extremist to see it. Millions of women get pregnant in this country every year. Do you know how many of them allow a person in a white coat to kill their babies?

BEN: I really don't want to debate this with you. It was better when we were talking about assassination, honestly.

JAY: We *are* talking about assassination. The objections to war are poisoned by this hypocrisy. About twenty percent. Twenty percent of all pregnancies in this country end up being aborted. That's hundreds of thousands of infants.

BEN: Fetuses.

JAY: Not fetuses! "Fetus" is a scientific word

that's deliberately chosen to be ugly so that the remorse of killing will not attach to it. Infants.

BEN: Nnn.

JAY: If it's an aphid, fine. When they're as big as a mouse, when they've got hands, they deserve our protection. They've become civilians.

BEN: Nnn.

JAY: That's the link. I'm marching with all these people against the war, and I'm screaming, "Hey Bush, what do you say? How many kids have you killed today?" And it's true, the blood is on his hands, so you scream it and scream it, but then it kind of sticks in your throat, you know? Because you look around at the screaming people in the crowd and you know damn well that they would shun you, they would turn all their fierceness and their fury on you if they knew that you believed that abortion was murder. They would! You know I'm right.

BEN: People get fierce about this, Jay, because, you know—

JAY: What?

BEN: Because in the old days women died.

JAY: Ah.

BEN: There were desperate women who went to

back-alley doctors who did terrible things. And they died.

JAY: Because there were evil doctors and incompetent doctors, and people who pretended to be doctors but were really killers, who harmed desperate women, therefore we must continue to permit the deliberate killing of the unborn? What kind of an argument is that? That's not an argument, that's a piece of shit!

BEN: No, it's not a piece of shit.

JAY: Yes it is. It's like saying, Because Saddam gassed his own citizens, we had to drop bombs that would kill his citizens so that he could be removed from power.

BEN: I don't see that they're parallel at all.

JAY: What the left is all about is equality before the law. If you're arrested for DUI, you can't have your father fix it for you. You can't send a cruise missile into a restaurant because you think a dictator is having dinner there with his family. And if you're pregnant and you would rather not be, you can't hire somebody with a suction machine to destroy your kid. It's as simple as that. The laws of the land apply to evil people, to good people, to old people, to unborn people. That's why babies are so

CHECKPOINT

beautiful, we feel how vulnerable and helpless they are. The medical profession has cut this link. They've sterilized our instincts.

BEN: People I know very well have had abortions.

JAY: I'm sure that's true.

BEN: I know them very, very well. They're not happy about it, they grieve over it.

JAY: Grief, now that's truth—they've got something there.

BEN: Well, they grieve. That's all I'll say.

JAY: You remember Sarah, the one with the bracelets? The doctor said she probably couldn't get pregnant because when she was young she'd had two abortions. Scar tissue. Now, she suffered over that. Don't you think some of the kids, the soldiers, over in Iraq who get caught in some sudden riot and fire off a round, and then they see that they just shot some six-year-old boy who's now dead on the sidewalk, don't you think they're going to grieve later on? Some of them? Try to figure out a way to tell themselves that their life is part of some larger good even though the most memorable thing they ever did was to shoot that boy dead in the street? Don't you think they're going to feel guilt?

BEN: Some of them will.

JAY: They definitely will. It's wrong for the government to do that to people, to put them into a position where some of them will do things that are obviously totally wrong and that they will recognize to be wrong later. And it's wrong for us to allow women to live with that grief for the rest of their lives. That was their one child, maybe. Maybe that was the baby that they were meant to have, and there weren't going to be any others.

BEN: You've obviously thought a great deal about this, and that's fine, and what I would recommend is that you—well, you know what I'm going to say.

JAY: What?

BEN: I was going to say, Why don't you get yourself a notebook, one of those little composition books with the marble design on the covers, and write all this down? Just for your own personal clarification.

JAY: It's intertwined. I get jittery when I try to write, I go here, I go there. I have to emit the words at normal talking speed. To somebody. When I go "Word, word, word, word" it doesn't make any sense. That's why they leave me. I wear people out.

BEN: Are you able to read at all?

JAY: Some, sure. Not like I used to, but sure, I go to Barnes & Noble, absolutely. I went a couple of weeks ago, had a cup of coffee. God, I'm parched. Shouldn't we break out a couple of these little bottles? Clinky clinky?

BEN: Not with you talking about this "path" of yours. Put that back. Put it back, Jay, I'm not kidding. You know what I tell my students to do?

JAY: What?

BEN: Some of them are upset about the war, their brains are addled. I say pick a book that you admire. Pick any book. Get a notebook and start copying it over. Copy the book from cover to cover. It's like running a flax comb through your mind. You card the wool.

JAY: Copy it?

BEN: Yes, start at the beginning and go right through to the end. Don't skip. You'll become the world's expert on that book.

JAY: Do you do that?

BEN: Sure. Well, I used to. I probably should again.

JAY: What books did you copy?

BEN: Let me think back. A book called *The Oregon Trail*. I copied that whole thing over one summer in Bermuda. I learned to write very very small because I didn't have that much paper. It was a lovely time.

JAY: How many pages was it?

BEN: I don't know, three hundred.

JAY: Really. Wow. When was this?

BEN: I spent a summer with my grandmother. It was hot, it was a sauna, and the cockroaches are big there. You been to Bermuda?

JAY: No.

BEN: The cockroaches are big, and the spiders, yike, they're like huge crabs, they're red and white. But it was nice. So I would sit all morning copying out Francis Parkman, and then I'd go for a swim, come back, have lunch, and then toward twilight my grandmother had her evening battle with the roaches. She had a tremor in her hand and when she used the bugspray I'd hear it, in the stillness, *fft-fft-fft-fft-fft-fft-fft*. She didn't have enough finger strength to really press the spritzer down and hit the roach with a full dose. So hours later, in the middle of the night, I'd wake up to this sound, turn on the light, and there was the poisoned roach in its death agony, upside down, beating its wings along the baseboard.

JAY: I've seen that.

BEN: But here's what I realized. There were plenty of roaches around when Francis Parkman was writing *The Oregon Trail*. There were roaches around when all those Dutch landscape artists were painting their landscapes. Ruisdael and Hobbema.

JAY: The smaller kind of roach, I believe, not those biggies.

BEN: It doesn't matter. The painters were doing the things that they could do, never mind about the pests—the pests were bracketed off. They didn't impinge. The painters looked at the trees. That's what you've got to do.

JAY: Maybe. I did—

ROOM SERVICE: Room service!

JAY: Ah, that's lunch.

BEN: Thank God.

JAY: Coming!

ROOM SERVICE: Good afternoon, gentlemen. How are you this afternoon?

JAY: Great, thanks, how are you?

ROOM SERVICE: Fine, thank you. On the table, gentlemen?

JAY: Yes, perfect, right here.

ROOM SERVICE: If you would please sign both.

JAY: Two and seven is nine, eight and four. There you go. Thank you.

ROOM SERVICE: Thank you very much, have a nice afternoon.

JAY: Ah! Here's your steak, man. They didn't give me any ketchup. Damnation.

BEN: Here's some.

JAY: Oh, great. Thanks. So you sat there in the heat copying out that book?

BEN: Sweat trickling off the backs of my hands, but yes, I copied it out, and it really taught me a lot. Mmmm, tasty.

JAY: Isn't that good steak? Peppercorn steak.

BEN: Dee-licious.

JAY: They have a good cook down there. Is it done medium?

BEN: It's medium. Bang on. You were right. Hits the spot.

JAY: Good. You want some of my fries?

BEN: Sure, I'll take a fry, thanks.

JAY: We need wine, at least. They've got a bottle here called Bella Firenze. Sounds a little bogus, but what do you say?

BEN: What time is it?

JAY: A quarter to two.

BEN:  Is it that late?

JAY:  Yep, yes it is.

BEN:  Well, a glass of wine can't hurt. This is on me, all right? I'll settle it with them downstairs.

JAY:  Okay, thanks. So I did go to Barnes & Noble a couple of weeks ago.

BEN:  Did you?

JAY:  Yeah, and I browsed around, and I went to the American history section. Oh, first I went to a section called True Crime. Lots of murders of women. There's obviously an appetite out there for murders of women. Slashing and killing of women. It's really odd, the hunger for it.

BEN:  Do you read those books?

JAY:  No way. What's the point? I can't muster the tiniest amount of interest in the particulars of some killer's life. They're mostly just dumb people who happen to have a violent streak. I mean, look at the president. I stick to the history section. You know there's a glossy new book on the Kennedy assassination?

BEN:  I can't say it surprises me.

JAY:  Supposedly Lyndon Johnson did it.

BEN:  Johnson did it? I thought it was the mob.

JAY:  It changes from day to day.

BEN: Listen, you're spending way too much time in the wrong parts of the bookstore. Forget the books. You need a nice long break. You need some gentleness and some love. Just like that good old Grace Slick said.

JAY: I've got to find somebody to love?

BEN: Yes, you do.

JAY: I agree. I feel like an asteroid. I'm so far out I'm somewhere beyond the Kuiper belt. But I think I first have to get rid of this impulse.

BEN: Yeah, well, get rid of the impulse.

JAY: By acting on it.

BEN: No, just get rid of it. Rid yourself of it.

JAY: No, Ben, what the man stands for is this whole entire tradition of blood and greed and bullshit. Blood, greed, and bullshit! Dietrich Bonhoeffer, think of him. A mild-mannered person, and he sees Hitler and he decides the only right thing to do is to kill the guy. There's a point beyond which even Dietrich Bonhoeffer has to act.

BEN: You think Bush is as bad as Hitler?

JAY: No, he's not. Of course he's not as bad as Hitler. But we've reached a point beyond the normal— We've reached a point of intolerability.

And he's escalating. And we've got these new scandals just popping up like daisies. We've got to shut the man down.

BEN: Shut him down—you sound like Kissinger.

JAY: Excuse me?

BEN: Think of your kids. Why aren't you there with them? Why aren't you being a father to them? You need to take a look at that.

JAY: Come on, I love those kids. I know, I know I'm too much of a naysayer, I know that.

BEN: You can't naysay all the time, it's deadly. I have to be careful about it myself. It's not fair to Julie.

JAY: Lousy naysayers, always down on life.

BEN: When we were in high school, did we sit around on our beanbag chairs thinking about the Vietnam War? Plotting how we would take bayonets to Richard Nixon? No. We did our chemistry homework.

JAY: You did, I didn't.

BEN: We read the books Mrs. Hunsell assigned. *Point Counter Point*, remember?

JAY: God, that was awful. Deadly stuff.

BEN: We listened to all that Zappa. "What will you do when the label comes off—"

JAY: "And the plastic's all melted, and the

chrome is too soft?" I believe we smoked a joint or two.

BEN: I believe we did. But were your parents always talking about the war? Mine weren't.

JAY: No, mine weren't, either.

BEN: I just wonder if they had spent every evening upset over that war—and you know, there was plenty to be upset about, there were the atrocities, My Lai, there was Operation Ranch Hand. Would it really have been better for us to have been raised in a state of constant misery over that war?

JAY: No, you're right, I had a good childhood. I made a few mistakes, everyone does. Totally fucked myself up later on. My poor mother. Remind me what Operation Ranch Hand was?

BEN: Oh, the defoliation. Agent Orange.

JAY: Right. More Bella?

BEN: I probably should switch over to coffee. But yeah, hell, give me a little more. You know, you're mellower now, I think. Or am I imagining things? You don't have that squinty look. Where's the gun?

JAY: Mmm? Oh, it's available. And I know a way in through the fence. One of the corners.

BEN: You won't get fifteen yards, man. You

might as well give me the gun and let me shoot you right now. Save yourself a walk.

JAY: I think I've got a fifty-fifty chance.

BEN: What can I say that'll make you stop? Whistle the theme to the *Andy Griffith Show*?

JAY: Not now, please.

BEN: What if I threw this glass at your head? Would that be a good idea?

JAY: No.

BEN: Then, when you ducked, I'd knock you down with the chair, maybe.

JAY: Don't do anything like that. I'm jumpy enough as it is.

BEN: Here's an idea. Just a suggestion, okay?

JAY: Okay.

BEN: And, you know, you can take this for what it's worth because it's not like my life is some shining example of how to live a life.

JAY: I know that.

BEN: But my suggestion is, get yourself a camera.

JAY: That's your suggestion? Get myself a camera. Sure thing. Take some pictures of our nation's capital, great. Heh heh heh.

BEN: No, I mean it, it's been an enormous help to me.

JAY: It's just that there's no time now. The marination—it's complete. This is the day.

BEN: I know what I'll do, I'll give you my—well, I'll loan you my camera. How about that?

JAY: Thanks, but I don't need to take pictures.

BEN: You don't have to take any pictures. Honestly, you'll enjoy just loading the film. The rolls of film are exactly the same shape as they were back when George Eastman's engineer first designed them a hundred years ago. Back then they were called cartridges—they looked like shotgun cartridges. Now it's called one-twenty film.

JAY: Is it expensive?

BEN: Yeah, it's pretty expensive, but it's worth it—the grain is so fine now. So when you can't stop thinking about the war, about how evil George W. is, how corrupt Cheney is, all that—all of which is true—but when it's paralyzing you, and you're not doing anything but thinking about the horror and the gangrene, load some film and go outside. Is there a park near where you're living?

JAY: There's a little green spot, yeah.

BEN: Fine, so go there. You might see, oh, I don't know, a nuthatch on a fence. You think, take the picture? No, no. There's somebody's cat, sniffing at a blade of grass. Take the picture? No, no. You move on. A twisted piece of wire on the ground. Yes? No, no. You see what's happening?

JAY: I'm not sure I do.

BEN: What's happening is that the weight of the camera in your hand—and remember, it's a heavy camera—the holding of it is changing the way you look at everything. You look up at the buildings, the stonework up there—ah, and then you see the trees. You put your eye to the viewfinder, and you're in the lens.

JAY: You're in the lens?

BEN: Exactly, you're in the lens. And then you focus. That's the great moment, when you turn the barrel of the lens and all the little wisps of fog sharpen a little, sharpen some more, and become parts of a tree. All these branches branching off.

JAY: The trees really get to you, eh?

BEN: Especially the old twisted ones. The last couple of months I must have shot, oh, maybe a dozen different trees. It's best to get to them before their leaves are out, so that you can see the whole structure.

JAY: I guess I'm out of luck, then.

BEN: No, no, leaves can be good, too. Leaves are good. Oh, but there was this one enormous catalpa tree a couple of miles from our house. It was kind of a wet, misty day, and I walked up to it, and I went "Whoa," and I brought it into focus and the whole thing just came alive for me in the viewfinder. It was an incredible explosion of black twigs reaching in every direction. I was down to maybe a thirtieth of a second, and I squeezed the trigger—

JAY: The trigger?

BEN: I mean the shutter, the little button.

JAY: You're as messed up as I am.

BEN: Anyway, I squeezed it, and the camera kind of shuddered. See, there's a heavy mirror in there that has to flip out of the way, so it kicks a little when you take the picture. But very fast. *Cloonk*.

JAY: Heavy but fast.

BEN: Yep, and I knew I had that catalpa in the bag. I knew its secrets. Yet there it was still out on the street for everyone else to enjoy. So who cares then about George W.? He's irrelevant. He's irrelevant. You see?

JAY: It's kind of funny—I hate to say it, but you know what all this makes me think of?

BEN: What?

JAY: The Sixth Floor Museum.

BEN: What's that?

99

JAY: You don't—? Oh, that's the museum at the Texas School Book Depository, in Dallas.

BEN: You went there?

JAY: I did indeed. They have a row of cameras under glass there—all the cameras that people were using on the day of the assassination. The old home movie cameras, and a kind of Polaroid camera that took a picture of a blob that supposedly was a person in a bush on the Grassy Knoll, but it's really a blob. In fact, it isn't even a blob anymore, because the Polaroid has faded, so all they've got is this enhancement. But the row of cameras is great, it's like a memorial. And you look at them for a little bit, and you nod, and then you walk over to the corner of the floor—the sixth floor—and you stand in the place where supposedly the guy aimed his rifle and shot the president.

BEN: I see.

JAY: They've got the boxes of schoolbooks piled up so that it looks pretty much the way it did. To me, frankly, it seemed like a very awkward vantage point. There were two guys there who were hunters, and one of them said, "Lord, that's one tough shot." They talked about how slow the car was moving, and the other guy said, "All I can say is, I sure couldn't make that shot." They were talking softly, you know, and for a moment we were all thinking like assassins.

BEN: Why did you go there?

JAY: It was last year, just around this time last year, I took the bus all the way from Birmingham to Dallas. There's a great bus station in Dallas, it's practically untouched, classic Deco lines, the Greyhound station. Just the way it would have looked, at least on the outside, in 1963.

BEN: But what made you take the bus there?

JAY: It was that thing I read on the Net, the news story. It was so awful.

BEN: About what?

JAY: It was in the *Sydney Morning Herald*.

BEN: Sydney, Australia?

JAY: Yes.

BEN: What was the story?

JAY: Oh, it was about this checkpoint, and, um. I don't want to—oh, it was a thing that happened, that nobody would have ever wanted to happen. But it happened, and it made me so mad. So mad at him.

BEN: Why don't you tell me.

JAY: It was just an event. Well. Okay. There were a bunch of Army guys there and this Land Rover drove toward them. It was filled with a family, they were fleeing. Many children. Everybody was jammed into this car, and they were trying to get out of the war zone.

BEN: Okay.

JAY: And they waved, and somebody at the checkpoint misinterpreted the wave, and so there was a huge blast of fire, and one of the women in the car, the mother, she said, "I saw the—" Sorry.

BEN: It's okay.

JAY: She said, "I saw the heads—" Pull myself together.

BEN: It's all right.

JAY: She said, "I saw the heads of my two little girls come off." That's what she fucking said. I'm not kidding you, man. "My two little girls." That's what she fucking said. Can you imagine it? You're just trying to get your family out of a war zone? Your farm's already been blasted by helicopters, and then a bunch of guys in Kevlar open fire on your kids, and you see that happen? Ho, God.

BEN: That's bad.

JAY: Liberators. Such bullshit. It's just one event. The grandfather was killed, too. You know what he had on? He was wearing a pin-striped suit so that he would look more American. Ho, man. Ho, man.

And that *creep,* that fucking Texas punk, who can't even talk, with his drugged-out eyes, he brought us to this point, to this war, and for nothing, for not one red fucking *thing.* And I thought, I want to see what it feels like to be in the last place where a president was shot dead. Where somebody had moved from the fantasy stage over to the reality stage, shall we say. So I took the bus there. And I stood there. And I thought, Man, there's no way I could do this. Too sharp an angle.

BEN: Good. That's good! That's good!

JAY: The feeling ebbed a little, and then a couple months ago it began to build again. Fallujah. Marine snipers on the roofs, shooting at everything. At ambulances. At children. Shooting at an old woman holding a white flag. Mosques hit. F-16s again, flames everywhere. And Kufa, boys with shrapnel wounds. Six people in a family died there, three children. And the prisons. The mockery on the guards' faces. It's like when he was governor of Texas, smirking over the executions. The man's personality trickles down through the entire military hierarchy and makes everyone meaner and nastier.

BEN: Including you.

JAY: Including me. And nobody around him is saying, Stop. Pull the Army out, get the Delta Force out, get the SEALS out, get the Green Berets out, get the CIA out, get the Marine snipers out, get the F-16s totally the fuck away from that part of the world. Right now. Yes, cut and run. Get away from that country that you have so royally fucked up. You know? Nobody's saying it to him. So then the desire for justice just starts moving through me. It's like a huge paddlewheel, it just churns up all of this foam and fury. VENGEANCE.

BEN: Please don't stand up! I mean it, this will invalidate any point you will ever want to make.

JAY: This *is* the point that I want to make. You're blocking me.

BEN: You'll just become another nutcase. What if I knock you out with this bottle?

JAY: Don't.

BEN: And what if coincidentally tonight, while you're out cold, somebody else shoots him, and tomorrow morning you wake up and you read the headline, and it says, you know, CRAZED MAN WIGS OUT AND SHOOTS PRESIDENT? I mean, what would your reaction be?

JAY: Now, that's a good question, that's a very good question.

BEN: Would your reaction be that this was a good thing? Remember what's happening tomorrow, okay, Cheney's on TV from some hideout, the stock markets are tumbling, the, um—

JAY: The stock markets? They're all just Styrofoam pellets. They're just big boxes of Styrofoam popcorn, that's what stocks are.

BEN: In any case, the day after, are you going to think, Ah, good, he did that, so I don't have to?

JAY: I'm going to think, I wish he hadn't done that. I wish I'd done that. Because this is the one thing that I have to contribute.

BEN: You're going to have other things. You will. Be patient.

JAY: Let me ask you. I'm going to go down there now and I may well get hit before I make it very far. But I may not. There's a hole in the fence. I've seen it, I know it's there, and I'm just going to RAM my way through that fucking hole. And I'm going to be out there on that lawn, and I'm going to run like a crazy man with my gun and my hammer. And those guys on the roof, you know? Here's the thing. The chances that somebody is going to be running toward the White House at any given moment are practically zero. They're like the people at the bomb-detection machines at the airport. There's no

**105**

chance that they're ever going to find a terrorist. So even though every piece of their training says to look for the danger signs, they know that there are no danger signs. Okay. So I'm counting on that. The guy's working his way through a bag of Skittles up there. His job is so awful. His job is to sit on the roof day after day, squinting at nothing. I mean, of all the pointless things to spend your life doing. Not only that, maybe he doesn't even like the president. Maybe the president spoke sharply to him one time. Or maybe he loves him. Anyway, he's beginning to have his doubts about the war. So he's not as attentive.

BEN: He's—

JAY: So I push my way through. I break out across the green, no cover, but I'm sprinting, and I'm fast, and I'm going to make it.

BEN: Then what? You're still outside.

JAY: Then, with my hammer, I smash my way through the windows. And then I leap in. I wave at Condoleezza. "Stick to the piano, baby!"

BEN: And then you're shot, and you fall.

JAY: Maybe, maybe not. But here's my question for you. Say I'm down, I'm bleeding on the rug, but I've got the gun under me and I've got just enough strength left to point it toward him—won't part of you think, He's got it coming to him? Huh?

BEN: I don't—

JAY: Won't you think to yourself, Man, I hope that little peckerfuck gets it right between the eyes?

BEN: I don't—I'm not—I can't predict how I would react if the president were actually shot.

JAY: You know part of you would celebrate.

BEN: I think that the simple sight of any human being stilled, you know—dead—that there's a basic patheticness to that. There's just a sadness or a stillness of one's emotions that comes from their not being able to speak, that is so, so . . . I don't want to say "sobering," but so quieting. So that, no, I don't think I'd feel any need to celebrate. Much as I dislike the guy. In fact I think I would feel a certain amount of horror knowing that to an extent I was part of it. To an extent I had something to do with it because I'd talked to you about it at length, and I'd failed. I wasn't successful in convincing you not to do it.

JAY: Don't be so hard on yourself.

BEN: But don't you think that if you—I mean, you've seen the tape of when Kennedy was shot. You've seen the frames that were cut out of the film because all that blood is blasting from his head? A spray of brain? I mean, it's a horrifying sight. It's a human being that is now just nothing. You want to be a part of that?

JAY: That's the thing. I have allowed myself to feel that feeling with the people in Fallujah, in Karbala, in Nasiriyah, in Basra, in Baghdad, in Mosul—all these cities. And Afghanistan before that. I've seen the pictures. And I feel that they—I mean Bush, any Marine sergeant, any soldier—all these guys are in the war business, one way or another. So they know that there's a certain risk involved. You can become a casualty of the wars you incite, or that you volunteer for. But these kids who are having their limbs blown off, they don't even know what's going on. There's just a sudden sound of the jet engines. Have you ever heard a Warthog?

BEN: I don't think so.

JAY: Well, they make this sound. *Arrw.* It's a kind of a walrus sound, almost, it's really disturbing. *Arrw.* I don't know if it's some sort of adjustment that the engines do as they're descending, but it's a fearful sound, it's like a giant swallowing. And you know, here are some kids playing in a street, they hear this walrus sound, and suddenly there are bits of really hot metal flying through the air. They look down in surprise and their own blood is coming out, and they're feeling cold. And they're dying fast. They don't know what's going on. They can't even explain to themselves what happened. They're noncombatants. They're innocent, they're innocent even of the knowledge that they are innocent. They're people just living their lives, and now their lives are over.

BEN: It hurts.

JAY: I can't stand it, Ben! I can't! I have to do something! You hear the man giving one of his radio addresses, and he has that way he has of slurring his words, as if he's drunk but he's not—"Housing sales are at an all-time high"—and you think of the war in the streets over there and of him tearing down what's left of the country, and you feel murderous, just MURDEROUS!

BEN: Feel murderous, by all means. Rage inwardly. Just don't actually attempt the murder. That's the dividing line.

JAY: Okay, well, I'm crossing it.

BEN: He's a person, try to remember that. A person's a person, as the good doctor said. He's a human being.

JAY: No, he's not, he's forfeited that status.

BEN: He really hasn't. He's got that sudden smile that he makes when he's answering a question. Have you seen it? It looks like he's not sure how he's going to finish the sentence, and there's a second of panic, his brow furrows, and then—ah!—he thinks of a word that he can plug in there. A big presidential word. He says it, and he flashes that childish smile of relief. It's a little moment of pride—"I made it, guys."

JAY: I see fear in his look sometimes. He knows what he's done.

BEN: I don't really think he does know, but he may sometimes have an inkling of how lost he is, how utterly at sea. So why'd you come here, Jay? To kill this person?

JAY: Why should he have a couple of hundred Secret Service men protecting him? Why does he deserve rocket launchers on his roof? Who was protecting those people in the Land Rover?

BEN: Nobody was. Nobody.

JAY: I can't understand why this outlaw, this FELON, who's killed something like twelve thousand people, should be alive when those girls are dead. It's just wrong. Not only is he alive, he's served coffee in special little fancy china cups, he's flown around in a big airplane with a living room in it, he's treated with round-the-clock, shit-eating deference! Reporters are out there in the Rose

Garden: "Mr. President? Oh, Mr. President? Tootle-ooh!" It's got to stop.

BEN: Where's this hammer of yours?

JAY: Under the comforter.

BEN: I don't see it.

JAY: Other side. Just fold it back.

BEN: Nice hammer.

JAY: Made in Brazil, do you see that?

BEN: Interesting. Yes, it's just as I thought.

JAY: What?

BEN: This is a special voodoo hammer.

JAY: Don't mess around, man. I'm not in the mood.

BEN: Bear with me. Let's take George W.'s picture from the box of bullets and place it faceup on a cushion. Like so. Where did you get the picture, by the way?

JAY: I got it off the White House website. It's an official photo.

BEN: Of course he's wearing the little flag pin.

JAY: Oh, that flag pin, it infuriates me. *Rrrrr!*

BEN: Now, this hammer is known as the Brazilian Mojo Hammer of Justice. Whatever harm you inflict upon an evildoer's image with this hammer will also be visited upon the evildoer himself.

JAY: I see. Okay.

BEN: So take a good smart whack at his forehead with it. Go on.

JAY: Just lay it on him?

BEN: Yes, put him out of his misery. He needs it. He needs that hammerblow in the middle of his forehead.

JAY: I'm a little hesitant.

BEN: Why?

JAY: I'm scared to do it!

BEN: Just lift the hammer. Good. Now when you bring it down, put your whole strength into it. Really kill him. Ready? Now, GO!

JAY: HHHHHHHRRRRRAAAAAAAGH! [*Flump!*]

BEN: And again?

JAY: DAMMIT! [*Flump!*] BASTARD! [*Flump!*] RRRRRRRAAAAGH! [*Flump!*]

BEN: Okay, okay. Wow. So how do you feel now? Any better?

JAY: No, I don't think so. Well, maybe I do. Actually I do feel a little better. Whoooo! Heh heh heh. For a second I almost felt like I was killing him. I really did, and I even felt sorry for him when I was killing him, that's the sick thing. He kept on smiling through it. His tie didn't budge.

BEN: No harm done to the cushion, I hope?

JAY: No, the picture's a bit torn, but that's to be expected. Whew, I'm a wreck.

BEN: See that? The only way to find out that you're not a killer is by killing the guy.

JAY: Yeah, but let's face it, all I really did was attack a picture. That's not justice. He's still wearing his flag pin every day. I want the man to crawl on his hands and knees down the streets of Baghdad saying, "I am so sorry, folks. I am so sorry that I put you through this. Just because I'm a reformed alcoholic and I needed a little war buzz, I destroyed your country, and I killed your families. And I am so fucking profoundly sorry for that." That's what he has to say. I won't rest till he says it. That will be true justice.

BEN: He can't very well say it if you've assassinated him, can he?

JAY: Hmm. That's an excellent point.

BEN: Where's your gun? Or do you not have one?

JAY: I told you I had a gun.

BEN: Tell me where it is, then.

JAY: The gun?

BEN: Yeah. Where is it?

JAY: It's in the closet.

BEN: Where?

JAY: Under the extra pillow.

BEN: Jesus, Jay, this is a gun!

JAY: I know.

BEN: Okay, listen, you freak, we're going to check out of here.

JAY: I can't, I've got all my stuff unpacked.

BEN: Pack it back up. Right now. Let's go. We're going to get out of Washington. This place isn't healthy for you.

JAY: I have a mission.

BEN: Your mission is over. Now move it, or I'll— I'll shoot you in the leg.

JAY: You're not capable of that.

BEN: Don't push me, I've had a very long afternoon. We're going to bury this gun somewhere. Ugh, it's got my fingerprints all over it. We're going to bury the bullets, too. And the hammer. We're going to get you home, you demented bum, we'll get you a chair, you can sit outside in the chair, I'll lash you to it, you can take your shoes off, put your feet in the grass. It's beautiful outside! I'll show you my camera. Now get packing!

JAY: Are you sure you don't want to take a little walk with me while we're in town? See the sights?

BEN: No.

JAY: We should at least drive by the White House. I could show you where I marched.

BEN: Absolutely not.

JAY: How about Dick Cheney's house? The vice presidential mansion, in all its stateliness. Hmmmmm?

BEN: No! Now pack up. And let's turn that thing off now.

JAY: You sure?

BEN: Really. Off. OFF.

JAY: All right, all right, all right, here we go. Over and out.

[*Click.*]

A NOTE ABOUT THE AUTHOR

Nicholson Baker was born in 1957 and attended the Eastman School of Music and Haverford College. He has published six previous novels—*The Mezzanine* (1988), *Room Temperature* (1990), *Vox* (1992), *The Fermata* (1994), *The Everlasting Story of Nory* (1998), and *A Box of Matches* (2003)—and three works of nonfiction, *U and I* (1991), *The Size of Thoughts* (1996), and *Double Fold* (2001), which won a National Book Critics Circle Award. He lives in Maine with his wife and two children.

A NOTE ON THE TYPE

This book was set in Minion, a typeface produced by the Adobe Corporation specifically for the Macintosh personal computer, and released in 1990. Designed by Robert Slimbach, Minion combines the classic characteristics of old style faces with the full complement of weights required for modern typesetting.